THE ART OF GAME COOKERY

By Rosemary Wadey

Eigil Larsen

1993 Edition

Published by Shooting Times for

HARMSWORTH ACTIVE

A division of Harmsworth Magazines Limited

THE ART OF GAME COOKERY

TOO often in the past, game has been shrouded in a certain mystique that meant many were discouraged from enjoying its unique qualities.

The aim of this book is to remove that uncertainty and illustrate how taking game from field to table really isn't as difficult as you might have feared.

There is so much to be gained from taking the trouble to get to know how best to enjoy the fruits of nature's harvest. Game meat is uniquely flavoursome, virtually fat-free and entirely natural.

The recipes we have gathered together celebrate the richness and diversity game has to offer – from a humble pigeon casserole to a magnificent and delicious venison en croute.

Whichever recipe tempts you most, you will find all are designed to appeal to both the novice and the more accomplished cook.

Bon appétit.

– Editor

Pigeon supreme with Madeira
(see recipe on page 37)

The Art of Game Cookery
By Rosemary Wadey
Additional information by Brian P. Martin
Edited by Barbara O'Flaherty
Food photography by Clint Brown

Design and production by Allan Davies at Harmsworth Active Design, 10 Sheet Street, Windsor, Berkshire, SL4 1BG. Reproduction, printing and binding by BPCC Wheatons Limited, Marsh Barton, Exeter, Devon.
The publishers would like to thank Salperton Park Estate which provided the backdrop for the recipe photography. The handmade china used for the photography in this book was supplied by Amanda Duncan.

Back cover picture by John Darling.

ISBN 1-873057-16-4

CONTENTS

INTRODUCTION
PREPARING YOUR GAME

POPULARLY the term 'game' applies to all wild animals, birds and some fish which are hunted, though in the eyes of the law 'game' means specific species. We have chosen the wider approach and set out to provide relevant details of the major species which are commonly eaten in Britain today. This book is a guide to all those who are involved with, or want to experiment with, game of all types, from the field to the table, from hanging, preparation and trussing through to the cooking and the eating.

SEASONAL ADVICE

Game supply and variety are restricted by law and most of the species dealt with in this book may be shot lawfully only at certain times of the year. Basically what this means is that gamebirds and wildfowl (duck, geese and waders) may be shot only during the autumn and early winter, but deer have a complicated set of seasons which vary according not only to the species but also to sex. Rabbits, hares and the woodpigeon have no 'close' season when they are protected from hunters for they are mostly regarded as significant agricultural pests; fortunately for us they are also very good to eat so that wastage is reduced to a minimum.

For further guidance on the game seasons, turn to our full list on page 158.

CHOOSING YOUR GAME

When offered for sale oven-ready game should be labelled as 'young', 'mature', 'casserole' and so on. This is an indication of suitability for roasting if young, otherwise it is advisable to cook by casseroling or in a pot roast, especially if no clue is given. However, for game in fur, feather and fin our identification guide on page 154 should help you further.

THE FIRST STEPS

If you don't fancy plucking and drawing the bird yourself, or don't have the time, then most poulterers and butchers will prepare your birds so they are 'oven ready' at only a small cost. Otherwise you will probably be able to find a friend who will help out – perhaps for an invitation to dinner to taste the result. This is particularly worthwhile if you have several brace to prepare for the freezer and simply feel you can't tackle the job on your own.

Most of the recipes ask for prepared or oven-ready game, so all is then set for the start of cooking. However, if you are not buying prepared game, your first step is to decide whether you will hang your game and for how long.

Always hang game in a cool, dry and well-ventilated place, away from flies. An outside shed is fine so long as it is in a cool position and provided it is not infested with mice or other unwelcome visitors. A brick outbuilding is better with a more uniform temperature. Hang birds by string tied around the neck of each bird or at least each brace, separately. Other game is usually hung by its feet.

A test of 'readiness' is if the tail feathers pull out easily; this may be after 2 days or up to 7 days. Even then, although the bird is ready for eating, many people will hang birds for considerably longer for the gamey flavour to increase. A greenish tinge on the skin below the breast will show the bird is really high. Hang birds purely to get the flavour *you* like and do not be influenced by those who insist only 'ripe' birds make good eating.

Older birds need longer hanging than young ones, but the temperature and humidity have a great influence over the time required. Warm, muggy conditions hasten the process greatly while cold and frosty weather will obviously slow everything down. Take care when it is really frosty that the birds do not begin to freeze, for that will of course stop the ripening process completely. Badly shot game should be used or cooked fairly quickly for it contaminates and deteriorates more quickly, often because the gut has been perforated. Always hang gamebirds still in the feather and undrawn.

The process of hanging is said to improve the flavour of the game, developing the characteristic 'gamey' flavour and at the same time helping to tenderise the bird. In tests, the best results for a full gamey flavour in pheasants were achieved after hanging for 9 days at $10^{o}C/50^{o}F$. However, where shot had perforated the gut, the ripening process was much more rapid. The conclusion was that shot birds should be hung so they cool as rapidly as possible and they should not be left

Preparing your game

in a pile during a shoot so the bacteria are not allowed to multiply too soon. Badly shot birds should be separated from the rest as they require a much shorter hanging time.

The ideal conditions for hanging are often not possible to achieve. But although a temperature of 10°C/50°F is recommended, cooler hanging for a longer period still produces a well-flavoured and tender pheasant. But remember to ensure that the place used for hanging is dry and cool with good ventilation and preferably with a through-draught of fresh air.

PLUCKING

On no account draw birds before plucking otherwise they will be difficult to handle. Start with the wings and then the neck and work downwards towards the tail. Cut off the wings at the first joint on small birds. Sometimes the wings are cut off completely, particularly if badly shot or very difficult to pluck as on the very small birds. Generally very little meat is lost if this is done, though presentation of the dish might be impaired.

Pluck out the feathers pulling them upwards and away from the position in which they naturally lie. Take care not to tear the skin by tugging at too many feathers at once for all game skin is tender and it should be preserved as much as possible as it offers the best protection to the flesh during cooking.

Tweak out the quill ends if tough by pinching between thumb and the blade of a small knife or use pliers, or tweezers for small ones. Singe the bird to remove the hair or down but be very careful not to scorch or burn the skin.

This process should *not* be done over a lighted gas flame on the cooker hob! Roll a piece of newspaper into a tight roll, take this and the bird outside and set light to the paper. This is then easily run all over the flesh without danger.

DRAWING

Use a small, sharp knife and cut off the head leaving about 10cm/4in of the neck (less on small birds). Put the bird on a table breast downwards. Start at the base and slit the skin of the neck down its whole length. Pull out the windpipe and crop using a damp cloth to get a good grip. Cut off the neck level with the body, pulling the skin aside and leaving a good flap of skin to fold over the back.

Turn the bird onto its back and slit between the tail and vent and remove the vent. Using two fingers, loosen the inside of the bird, being careful, by keeping the fingers close to the breastbone, not to break the gallbladder (very bitter tasting) which is attached to the liver. Gently draw out the gizzard and intestines, heart and liver with the gallbladder attached. The lungs are often more difficult to get at for they are hard up against the ribs. Do not fret if you are unable to remove every single scrap of the lungs, for it will not affect the flavour of the bird.

Cut off the toes, although in some game the feet and part of the leg can be cut off too. In old birds, if the sinews don't come away, thread a skewer between them, wind around and jerk them out sharply. Sinews left in the legs can make them tough and difficult to eat when cooked.

Dip the scaly part of the legs in boiling water and scrape off. Wipe out the inside of the bird with a clean damp cloth, but do not wash unless absolutely necessary.

TRUSSING

Pull the wings into place and plump up the legs. Tie string around the legs under the body. If using skewers thread the skewer first through the wing tip, plump part of the leg, then body, other leg and wing tip. Tie string around the legs as before and catch around the ends of skewers. Pull the neck skin well over and tuck under the string.

PREPARING INDIVIDUAL GAME
Pheasant

Hen pheasant is often preferred for eating as it is considerably smaller and more tender, but the cock bird is still excellent and stretches to feed more people. In any case you are likely to have both as pheasants are usually sold or given away in a brace which comprises one cock and one hen. The eyes should be bright, claws slender, spurs short and rounded - they become pointed and later hard and ragged with age. The first wing-tip feather is pointed and the upper part of the

Preparing your game

beak flexible in a young bird. The tail feathers should not come out easily. Hang for 7-10 days, or longer if preferred. For those who dislike a strong flavour prepare and cook as soon as possible but try at least to wait until the tail feathers come out easily or it may well be tough when cooked. It is thought by some that the oil in feathers helps the flavour of the bird.

Pluck carefully as the skin, especially on the breast, will tear easily, and keep some tail feathers for decoration of the roasted bird. These feathers can be put back into position to take to the table, if liked. Wipe the bird carefully inside and out with a clean damp cloth and then truss. Never wash inside unless absolutely essential.

To truss the bird, push the thighs back close under the wings and the body and then push a skewer through the wing tips, thighs and body. Loop string around the legs, tail and under the thighs to catch the skewer at each end and tie underneath.

Pheasant will serve 2-3 portions or 4 if very large.

Partridge

Young birds have pointed wing feathers and often yellowish or red legs (depending on the type). The feathers become rounded with age and the legs turn a blueish-grey.

Hang for 3-6 days depending greatly on the weather. Pluck draw and truss as for pheasant either using just string or string and skewer. Either leave the feet on or cut off the toes.

Retain the liver from the giblets, if possible, to put inside the bird with a knob of seasoned butter. Cover the breast with bacon or pork fat and, if available, add a vine leaf under the fat for flavour.

A partridge will serve one person generously.

Grouse

These should have bright eyes and supple beak and breastbone. Hang for 3-6 days, allowing longer in frosty weather, but leave for only a day or so if warm and muggy. Pluck grouse very carefully for the skin is even more tender than the other birds and will tear very easily. Draw as for all game and cut off just the toes. If preferred the feet can be cut off too. Truss as usual with or without skewers, put a knob of butter in

the cavity and the breast can be covered with fatty bacon or pork fat which should be removed for the last part of the cooking to brown up the breast.

A grouse will usually serve two people unless a very small bird.

Wild duck

All types of wild duck should hang for only 1-3 days before plucking for the oily flesh tends to become sour if kept too long. Deal quickly with birds whose feathers have become saturated in retrieving for example.

Pluck as for game or ordinary domestic duck. Draw carefully removing all the knobs of fat inside the cavity. Take care to singe for ducks have a lot of down which should be removed.

Truss like a domestic duck using skewers and string for mallard and just string for smaller birds. Season inside and out and cover lightly with softened butter. Remember unlike domestic duck, a wild duck is a dry bird so needs plenty of fat and basting.

One mallard serves 2-4 people, and a teal just one; but all the other duck serve 1-2 as a rough guide. It is always better to have too much than too little if you are unsure of the quantity. None of your guests will be disappointed and leftovers are delicious cold.

Preparing your game

Pigeon

These birds need not be hung at all, but if they are then it should be only for 1-3 days. Pluck, draw and singe (if necessary) as for other small feathered game, and simply tie the legs in place with string.

Often the wings are cut off completely for ease of plucking, and, if only the breasts are to be used, it is simpler to cut the skin across the breastbone and pull off the skin and feathers all in one go.
See picture below.

Wild goose

Pluck birds taking care to remove the stump ends of the quills from the wings and singe thoroughly to remove the down. Cut off the feet and wing tips at the first joint. Cut off the head and draw as for other game. Clean inside the bird with a clean damp cloth - and again do not wash.

To truss, use a long skewer and pass through the wing, body and wing again. Pass a second skewer through the end of the wing joint through the thickest part of the leg, through the body and out again through the leg and wing tip the other side. Fold the neck skin under and then tie string around all the skewer ends to secure the joints and neck skin.

In the case of the woodpigeon (left) it is often easier to cut along the breastbone and remove the prime meat either side. (Picture by Philip Upton)

Plucking a pheasant (pictured far left) involves drawing out the feathers in a swift, sure movement against the direction of growth. (Picture by Graham Downing)

Snipe and Woodcock

Woodcock should be plump and supple but not flabby. Feathers beneath the wings should be like down, and the feet supple in young birds. They are usually hung for just 1-2 days if to be cooked undrawn or for 3-5 days if drawn. Snipe need no hanging and can be eaten undrawn.

Pluck both birds as usual but also pluck the head completely. Singe all over carefully and then remove the skin from the head and neck and, with a sharp knife, take out the eyes. From the side of the bird, beside the thigh, make a small cut and remove the intestines.

Cut out the crop from a small cut made in the neck. Wipe the birds outside and inside where possible with a clean damp cloth; to truss, twist the head around and, using the beak as a skewer, pass it under the wings, through the legs and into the body. Tie the feet together with string. These birds can also be drawn (more usually woodcock) and stuffed if preferred, but this is not the traditional way to prepare and serve them. Similarly there is no reason why the head should not be removed as with larger gamebirds, if preferred.

Hare

Hare should be hung unpaunched for 6-8 days to improve the flavour. Hang it by the hind feet and place a small bowl under the nose to catch the blood, which is then used to thicken and flavour the gravy or sauce with which the hare is served.

A hare is usually skinned and then paunched – the opposite to the procedure with a rabbit.

To skin, cut off the feet at the first joint. Loosen the skin around the back of the legs. Hold the end of one leg and bend at the joint so the flesh can then be grasped and the skin pulled off. Do the same with all the legs. Cut off the ears and pull the skin off the head and the rest of the body with the help of a small, sharp knife. Take out the eyes.

To paunch, lay the hare on paper and then with scissors snip the skin at the fork and cut it up to the breastbone. Open the paunch by cutting carefully through it. Draw out the entrails. Reserve the kidneys. Detach the liver taking care not to puncture the gallbladder, then cut out and discard the gallbladder

Preparing your game

and the flesh around it. Cut the diaphragm and draw out the lungs which should be discarded and then find the heart and retain.

Catch the accumulated blood in the basin. Wipe out with a clean damp cloth.

To truss, cut the sinews in the hind legs at the thighs, bring forward and press closely against the body. Bend the forelegs in the same way.

Fix with two metal skewers and, if necessary, tie into place with fine string. Hare is probably more often jointed and this is done in the same way as for rabbit.

Rabbit

These should be paunched as soon as killed or within a few hours, preferably not more than 12 hours. Hang by the feet for 1-3 days before skinning. A blueish tinge to the rabbit indicates that it is stale. Rabbit should be paunched and then skinned.

To paunch, make a slit the length of the stomach. Slide out the entrails and discard everything except the liver. Take care to remove the intestine and formed faeces near the tail. Wipe out with a clean cloth and hang.

To skin, cut off the ears and all the feet at the first joint. Loosen the skin from the flesh along the slit made from paunching and working towards the hind legs gently strip off the skin, pulling it inside out. Turn the rabbit over and remove the rest of the skin, freeing the front legs and then the head, using a sharp knife. Remove the eyes.

Clean the rabbit carefully. Remove the kidneys, then break the diaphragm membrane and lift out the heart and lungs. Keep the heart, discard the lungs and keep the kidneys and liver.

Wash the rabbit well in salted water and, if liked, soak in salted water or cold water with vinegar added for $1/2$-1 hour to remove any strong flavour. This soaking is not absolutely necessary, only a matter of preference.

To truss, tie the rabbit with string so that it is in a sitting position with string around the legs as necessary. However, rabbit is more often jointed before cooking, keeping the forelegs whole, back legs whole or in two pieces and the back in four or five pieces. The head can be split or discarded.

JOINTING
Gamebirds

Use either a sharp knife or poultry shears. To halve the birds simply cut along the breastbone and then around and along the backbone. The backbone itself may be left on one portion or be removed altogether. For quarters cut each half into two keeping the breast and wing on one piece and the thigh and drumstick on the other. For grilling game it is usual to halve the birds or spatchcock them. To spatchcock, cut the bird down the backbone and press open flat; to keep the bird flat for grilling insert a crisscross of two wooden skewers to keep and hold the shape. Remember to remove them before serving.

Hare and rabbit

Cut off the legs; leave the forelegs as they are and cut the hind legs in half at the joint. However for smaller rabbit the hind legs may be left whole. The back is cut into even-sized pieces of 4-5 for rabbit and 5-8 for hare, again depending on size. The head may be left whole, split in half or more usually discarded. For a saddle of hare or rabbit, remove the legs and trim off or fold under the loose flaps from the stomach, leaving the length of the back as the saddle.

Venison

The jointing of venison is best left to someone who knows how to butcher an animal or you may well ruin the best cuts if you are not sufficiently 'in the know'. Once the meat has been hung, a butcher or gamedealer will often help and then the prime joints of haunch, loin, fillet and chops can be dealt with accordingly. Once this is done you can easily bone out the joints if you want to cook the meat boned and rolled, using a small sharp knife. The lesser cuts can be diced, sliced or minced ready for use.

BONING GAMEBIRDS

There are two main methods of boning a gamebird or indeed any type of poultry: firstly to produce a completely boneless and shapeless lump of skin and flesh; and secondly again a lump of skin and flesh but one which can be stuffed and reshaped into a bird again as the lower leg bones and wing bones are left in

Preparing your game

place to give balance to the bird. I prefer the part-boned method for serving both hot and cold.

Take a small sharp knife and cut off the wing tips and legs below the drumsticks. Make a cut through the skin along the backbone, then, working from the tail, gradually scrape the flesh from the carcase working towards the thigh. When you reach the thigh socket, break it and gradually work the flesh off the thigh bone and remove. Either stop there or continue and remove the drumstick. Continue removing flesh from the carcase until you reach the wing. Again break the socket joint and scrape the flesh off the top wing bone and remove. Leave at that or also remove the lower wing bones carefully. Return to the carcase and work off the flesh up to the breastbone.

Turn the bird round and complete the other side in the same way. Then carefully cut the flesh from the breastbone and lift out the carcase. Use the carcase and other bones for stock. Turn the piece of game so that it is back the correct way and lay skin-side downwards ready for stuffing. Pull the flaps of skin over the stuffing and secure with skewers or sew with fine string. Turn the bird over, reassemble the shape and tie into place. If all the bones are removed the leg and wing flesh is left inside the skin so the complete bird looks just like a roll of meat.

BONING GAMEFISH

Small fish are usually boned by first cutting along the stomach from head to tail (after gutting), then placing with the opening flat on the table. The thumb is then run very firmly along the length of the backbone several times until the bone becomes loose. Turn the fish over and gently ease out the main backbone with all the other bones still attached.

The other way is to cut out the bone; this is quicker but takes out more of the flesh with the bones and also leaves more parts of bone in the fish. To do this simply make a cut along the length of the backbone from head to tail of the fish keeping the knife flat and touching the bones as much as possible. Turn the fish over and repeat on the second side, then lift out the bones leaving the fish in one piece. Large fish are usually boned by the cutting method or are filleted and then reassembled, sometimes also after being skinned.

FILLETING FISH

Cut off the head and tail after gutting and then insert a sharp knife under the tail. Gradually cut the flesh from the bones, keeping as close to the bones as possible while working towards the head. Turn the fish over and repeat on the second side. If the fish slips, then scatter a little coarse salt on the preparing surface.

To skin the fish turn it so it is skin-side downwards and, beginning at the tail, slice the flesh from the skin keeping the knife at a slight angle, pressing firmly yet working along the fish towards the head at the same time.

Both of these processes sound complicated but become much easier with a little practice.

FREEZING

Freezing is an all important part of game preparation. For freezing use only fresh game. Take care with old, tough birds and if they are badly shot either cook at once, or cut into portions and only freeze the best of these.

Once the game is prepared it should be chilled until cooking time arrives. High game must be wrapped before putting in the refrigerator, otherwise everything else will probably pick up its flavour. Be sure also to place it at the bottom of the fridge so should it drip, it cannot do so on to anything else and contaminate it. If it is to be frozen it should be wrapped, labelled and either chilled immediately before freezing or be put straight into the freezing part of the freezer as soon as possible.

It is not a good idea to freeze very high game or that which has been badly damaged by shot for these tend to deteriorate during freezing. Neither is it recommended to freeze in feather or fur unless you have a freezer specifically set aside for this purpose.

Fish must be very fresh to freeze, almost straight from the water is best, and they must be wrapped and packed into the freezer with great care to make sure they keep a good shape during storage. Many people prefer to gut out the fish before freezing and if space is very limited then cut off the heads too.

Cooked game dishes freeze well and can be a boon for emergency meals that are a little bit different from the usual, but only store for a maximum of 3 months.

PHEASANT
BRITAIN'S FAVOURITE

PROBABLY the most popular and best known of British gamebirds. So much so in fact that many people think only of pheasant when game is mentioned and any other type of game sounds completely foreign to them. This is slowly changing, however, as many varieties of game become more widely available through the larger supermarkets – and if you can buy it at a supermarket then it must be all right and worth a try!

And of course there are many gamedealers and shops which stock game both fresh in season and frozen out of season.

Pheasants are at their best from mid-October to December. They should be hung after shooting otherwise older birds are likely to be tough and most birds will be lacking in flavour, but the length of hanging is a matter of very personal taste varying from 1-3 weeks. The average time for hanging is 7-10 days but in warmer and more humid weather the 'ripening' process will be much quicker while frosts and cold spells will slow it down.

A young cock bird will have round-ended, comparatively short spurs during its first year of life. In its second year they are a little longer and pointed but after that they become sharp and long, indicating that the bird is really mature and likely to be tough! The outer wing-tip feathers are pointed in a young bird but they become rounded with age. The young hen has soft feet which gradually harden and become rough as she ages.

Young pheasants are at their best when roasted but it is essential to pot-roast or casserole mature birds which can be really tough with sinewy, almost inedible legs. Some people are wary of the deep yellow fat found on some pheasants. Remove what you can and if you feel it will impair the flavour then either remove all the skin, taking the fat with it, and cook the bird in a sauce. In fact it is unlikely to impair the flavour unless perhaps the bird has been frozen with an excess of fat for a long time, when it will be the fat that turns rancid, spoiling the flavour of the pheasant. By adding a few pieces of raw onion and fresh herbs to the cavity, you will not notice any difference in flavour in a fresh pheasant.

A pheasant will serve 2-4 portions depending on size.

PHEASANT WITH LIME AND LEMON
(pictured opposite, recipe on page 25)

STIR FRY PHEASANT AND GINGER
(pictured below, recipe on page 24)

Pheasant recipes

BASIC ROAST PHEASANT

Probably the most popular way to serve this delicious gamebird.

> 1 pheasant, oven ready
> Knob of butter
> Quarter of lemon or orange or wedge of onion
> Melted dripping, butter or oil
> Salt and pepper
> Few rashers streaky bacon or piece of pork fat, beaten
> Little flour (optional)
> *To serve:*
> Fried breadcrumbs
> Bread sauce
> Game chips
> Watercress

Wipe the pheasant inside and out and place a knob of butter and a piece of lemon, orange or onion in the cavity. Truss lightly and stand in a roasting tin.

Pour melted dripping, butter or oil over the bird (or rub generously with softened fat) and season lightly, if liked; then cover the breast with bacon rashers or a piece of pork fat. Cook in a hot oven (220°C/425°F, Gas Mark 7) for $^{3}/_{4}$–$1^{1}/_{4}$ hours depending on the size of the bird, basting regularly until cooked through and tender.

The bacon or pork fat can be removed 15 minutes before ready, the breast dredged lightly with flour and basted; then return to the oven to complete the cooking and brown the breast. Unlike some game, pheasant should be properly cooked and not served slightly underdone.

Serve the pheasant on a warmed dish (with trussing string removed) garnished with watercress and game chips. Use the pan juices with surplus fat spooned off, to make a thin gravy and also serve fried crumbs and/or bread sauce and a green vegetable. Small potatoes may be roasted along side the pheasant.
SERVES 3-4 (depending on size)

Note: although the pheasant should be properly cooked, it should in no way be overcooked or the flesh will become dry, coarse and very uninteresting.

PHEASANT PUDDING

A good, sturdy meal fit for a cold day, and one to please those who like a steamed pudding!

> 1 pheasant, oven ready
> About 2 level tablespoons seasoned flour
> 12 streaky bacon rashers, derinded and rolled
> 1 onion, peeled and sliced
> 2 sticks celery, sliced
> 1-2 carrots, peeled and sliced
> Salt and pepper
> About 4 tablespoons stock, water, wine or cider
> $1/4$ level teaspoon ground coriander
> *Pastry:*
> 300g/10oz self-raising flour
> $1/2$ level teaspoon salt
> 100g/4oz shredded suet
> 1 level teaspoon dried thyme or mixed herbs
> Approx 175ml/6 fl oz cold water

Cut the pheasant into small pieces, discarding the boney carcase but don't take the flesh off the wings or drumsticks, simply cut through the joints. Toss in seasoned flour.

For the pastry sift the flour and salt into a bowl and mix in the suet and

BASIC ROAST PHEASANT

PHEASANT PUDDING

herbs. Add sufficient water to mix to a soft elastic dough and knead only lightly until just smooth.

Roll out about three-quarters of the pastry and use to line a greased 1-litre / $1^3/4$ -pint (approx) pudding basin, making sure there are no holes in the pastry. Layer up the pieces of pheasant, bacon rolls, and vegetables in the pastry-lined basin.

Season the stock or water and add the coriander, then pour over the pheasant. Roll out the remaining pastry for a lid, damp the edges, position, trim and press the edges very firmly together. Cover first with a layer of greased greaseproof paper with a pleat across the centre to allow for expansion, then either a lid or foil or a pudding cloth. Stand the basin in a pan of boiling water which comes halfway up the sides of the basin, cover and simmer gently for about 3 hours; adding more boiling water to the pan as necessary.

To serve, remove the coverings from the basin and serve either straight from the basin with a cloth tied round it or be brave and turn the pudding onto a plate! Serve with a white sauce.
SERVES 4

PHEASANT BEANPOT

Red kidney beans are an excellent addition to a casserole but they must be boiled well for at least 15 minutes and then well cooked until tender, for safety. Canned red beans may be used if preferred, simply drain and use a 425g/15oz can.

1 brace pheasants, oven ready
175g/6oz red kidney beans
25g/1oz butter or margarine
1 tablespoon oil

225g/8oz carrots, peeled and sliced
2 cloves garlic, crushed
1 level teaspoon oregano or marjoram
150ml/$1/4$ pint cider, chicken or game stock
Salt and black pepper
2 tablespoons wine vinegar
100g/4oz button mushrooms, halved
1 level tablespoon tomato purée
$1/4$ level teaspoon mild chilli powder
1 small cauliflower, cut into florets
To garnish:
Freshly chopped parsley

Cook the beans in plenty of boiling, unsalted water for about $1^1/2$ hours or until tender, making sure they boil really fast for 15 minutes. Drain. Melt the fat and oil in a frying pan and brown the pheasants all over. Transfer to a large casserole or roasting tin.

Add the carrots, garlic, herbs, cider and sufficient boiling stock to just cover the thighs of the birds. Season well, add the vinegar and cover tightly with a lid or foil. Cook in a moderate oven (180°C / 350°F, Gas Mark 4) for 1 hour. If using mature birds, allow $1^1/4$-$1^1/2$ hours. Add the drained beans, mushrooms, tomato purée and chilli powder, re-cover and return to the oven for 20-30 minutes. Meanwhile cook the cauliflorets in boiling salted water until tender-crisp, then drain.

To serve, put the pheasants on a large serving dish and surround with the drained beans and vegetables from the pot and the cauliflorets. Serve the strained cooking juices in a sauce boat. Sprinkle the vegetables with parsley.
SERVES 4-6

PHEASANT BEANPOT

Pheasant recipes

PHEASANT WITH WALNUTS AND CRANBERRIES

Mature pheasants are best cooked slowly in a casserole or braised to ensure they are tender; the flavour is excellent and often the birds are a little larger giving plenty for four portions.

1 tablespoon oil
25g/1oz butter
1 mature pheasant, oven ready
Salt and black pepper
1 large onion, peeled and sliced
4-5 sticks celery
1^{1}/$_{2}$ level tablespoons flour
Approx 300 ml/^{1}/$_{2}$ pint stock
150ml/^{1}/$_{4}$ pint dry white wine
75g/3oz whole cranberries, fresh or frozen
50g/2oz walnut halves

Melt the butter and oil in a pan. Cut the pheasant into quarters and season well. Fry quickly in the fat until browned all over and place in a casserole. Fry the onion and celery gently in the same fat until soft, but not coloured, then stir in the flour and cook for a minute or so.

Gradually add the stock and wine and bring up to the boil. Season well and pour over the pheasant. Cover casserole and cook in a moderate oven (180°C/350°F, Gas Mark 4) for 45 minutes. Adjust the seasonings, stir in the cranberries, walnuts and a little more boiling stock if necessary, replace lid and return to the oven for 20-30 minutes or until very tender.

Serve with jacket potatoes.
SERVES 4

Note: walnuts may be replaced with pecan nuts or cooked or reconstituted chestnuts, if preferred.

CRISPY PHEASANT WITH HOLLANDAISE SAUCE

Fried breadcrumb-coated pieces of pheasant with Hollandaise sauce.

4 raw pheasant breasts from young birds
Little French or tarragon and thyme mustard
8 rashers lean back bacon derinded
2 eggs, beaten
100g/4oz fresh white breadcrumbs
Deep or shallow fat for frying
Hollandaise Sauce:
4 tablespoons white wine vinegar
2 tablespoons water
8 peppercorns, crushed
4 egg yolks
175g/6oz butter, softened
Salt and pepper
Lemon juice to taste
To garnish:
Watercress and tomatoes

Remove the skin from the pheasant breasts. Spread a little mustard on the bacon and wrap around the pheasant securing with wooden cocktail sticks. Dip each piece in the beaten egg and then roll in the breadcrumbs. For a crisp and thicker coating, repeat the dipping in beaten egg and bread-crumbs and then chill for at least 30 minutes, or until required. Cook in hot deep fat (approx 160°C/325°) for 5-8 minutes or until golden brown and cooked through; or fry in shallow fat for about 10 minutes each side; or place on a greased baking sheet and cook in a fairly hot oven (200°C/400°F, Gas Mark 6) for 40 minutes until crispy. Drain on kitchen paper and serve hot with the Hollandaise sauce, tomatoes and watercress. For the sauce, put the vinegar, water and

PHEASANT WITH WALNUTS AND CRANBERRIES

CRISPY PHEASANT WITH HOLLANDAISE SAUCE

peppercorns in a saucepan, bring up to the boil and boil rapidly until reduced by half. Strain into a basin or the top of a double saucepan.

Beat in the egg yolks and if using a basin stand it over a pan of gently simmering water; cook gently until the sauce has thickened, stirring all the time. Gradually beat in the butter, a little at a time, until a coating consistently is obtained.

Season to taste and sharpen with a little lemon juice. Serve warm or cold.
SERVES 4

CRISPY PHEASANT WITH HOLLANDAISE SAUCE
(pictured left)

Pheasant recipes

POACHER'S PHEASANT

A boned-out pheasant may sound rather complicated, but if you follow the instructions carefully and use a small sharp knife there should be no problems – but have a little patience!

1 plump pheasant, drawn
450g/1lb pork sausagemeat
50g/2oz fresh white breadcrumbs
1 small onion, peeled and finely chopped
175g/6oz lean ham, diced
1/2 level teaspoon dried sage
100g/4oz button mushrooms, chopped
Salt and black pepper
1 small clove garlic, crushed
Few rashers streaky bacon, derinded
Butter or margarine
Sauce:
2 level tablespoons flour
1 level tablespoon tomato purée
300ml/1/2 pint good stock (made from the carcase)
150ml/1/4 pint red or white wine
2 tablespoons redcurrant, rowan or quince jelly
1 tablespoon lemon juice
Grated rind of 1/2 lemon
To garnish:
Watercress
Game chips

Turn the pheasant onto its breast and make a cut right along the backbone. Gradually ease the flesh off the carcase using a sharp knife until you come to the wing bone. Cut out the top bone of the wing leaving the rest as it is. Work on towards the leg and break at the socket joint; then ease out the top leg bone.

Continue all round the carcase until it can be removed. Lay the bird on a flat surface skin side downwards. Mix together the sausagemeat, breadcrumbs, onion, ham, sage, mushrooms, seasonings and garlic; shape into a block and lay on the pheasant flesh.

Put the edges together to enclose the stuffing and fold the neck flap over; secure with fine skewers or sew together with fine string. Turn the pheasant over and reshape the legs and wings, again securing with skewers or string.

Place in a roasting tin and if the skin is broken cover first with bacon and then spread with softened butter. Season and roast in a moderate oven (180°C/350°F, Gas Mark 4) for about 1 1/4 hours or until cooked through. Baste several times during cooking. Remove from the tin and keep warm.

Reserve 2 tablespoons of the pan juices in the tin and stir in the flour and tomato purée.

Cook for a minute or so then gradually add the stock and wine. Bring to the boil and simmer for 2 minutes.

Strain into a clean pan and stir in the jelly, lemon rind and juice and seasonings to taste.

Simmer for 2 minutes and then serve with the pheasant garnished with watercress and game chips.
SERVES 4-5

Note: pheasant cooked in this way is also excellent served cold either as it is or glazed with aspic jelly.

To carve: simply cut straight across the breast to reveal attractive slices of the stuffing surrounded by the pheasant meat.

PHEASANT VIN BLANC

A useful recipe for a young pheasant or several partridges, needing only creamed potatoes, rice or pasta as an accompaniment.

1 young pheasant or 2-3 partridges, oven ready
1/2 lemon, sliced
3-4 rashers bacon, derinded
1 onion, peeled and quartered
6 whole cloves
1 bay leaf
Salt and black pepper
150ml/1/4 pint white wine
150ml/1/4 pint stock
4 large carrots, peeled and sliced
4 sticks celery, sliced
1-2 level teaspoons cornflour

Place the lemon and bacon over the breast of the pheasant and secure with string or cotton. Place in flameproof casserole only a little larger than the birds and add the onion, cloves, bay leaf, seasonings, wine and stock. Bring up to the boil, cover and cook in a moderate oven (180°C/350°F, Gas Mark 4) for 30 minutes. Baste the pheasant and add the carrots and celery.

Replace the lid and return to the oven for a further 30 minutes or until tender and the vegetables are just cooked. Discard the onion, cloves and bay leaf and place the pheasant on a serving dish surrounded with the carrots and celery. Remove the bacon and lemon, if liked, and keep warm.

Thicken the juices with cornflour blended in a little cold water and bring back to the boil. Adjust seasonings and serve with the pheasant.
SERVES 2-4

PHEASANT AND BEEF PIE

Cooked pheasant meat, minced beef and vegetables make a delicious pie filling; and this is a good way to use up the legs from pheasants where the breasts are required for other recipes.

Cooked legs of 2 pheasants or
1 whole pheasant, roasted
225g/8oz raw minced beef
4 rashers bacon, derinded and chopped
1 onion, peeled and chopped
1 carrot, peeled and chopped
Salt and pepper
25g/1oz butter or margarine
25g/1oz flour
300ml/1/2 pint cider
225g/8oz shortcrust pastry (made using 225g/8oz plain flour etc)
Beaten egg or milk to glaze

Cook the mince, bacon, onion and carrot in a pan, with no extra fat, for about 10 minutes, stirring frequently. Season well and cool. Melt the fat in a pan, stir in the flour and cook for a minute or so. Bring up to the boil and simmer for 2 minutes. Add to the mince mixture. Strip the flesh from the pheasant, chop and stir into the mince; pour into a pie dish.

Roll out the pastry, cut a strip 2.5cm/1in wide and place on the dampened rim of the dish. Brush this rim with water and position the lid. Trim the edges, crimp and decorate the top with leaves made from the pastry trimmings. Glaze with beaten egg, make a hole in the top and bake in a fairly hot oven (200°C/400°F, Gas Mark 6) for about 45 minutes until the pastry is golden brown and filling piping hot. Serve hot or cold.
SERVES 5-6

PHEASANT VIN
BLANC

PHEASANT AND
BEEF PIE

Pheasant recipes

POT ROAST PHEASANT
WITH CHESTNUTS

Good for young and mature birds alike. The chestnuts give an excellent flavour and texture and blend well with the taste of the pheasant.

1 large or 2 smaller pheasants, oven ready
Salt and black pepper
1 tablespoon oil
25g/1oz butter or margarine
225g/8oz button onions, peeled

POT ROAST PHEASANT
WITH CHESTNUTS
(pictured right)

225g/8oz peeled chestnuts (see note below)
25g/1oz flour
150ml/^{1}/4 pint red wine
450ml/^{3}/4 pint stock
Grated rind or thinly pared rind of 1 orange cut into julienne strips
Juice of 1 orange
2-3 level tablespoons coarse orange marmalade
1 red pepper, deseeded and sliced

Wipe the pheasants all over and season with salt and pepper. Heat the oil and fat in a pan and fry the pheasant to brown all over. Transfer to a casserole.

Fry the onions and chestnuts in the same fat until lightly browned and then stir in the flour and cook for a minute or so.

Gradually add the wine and stock and bring up to the boil, stirring frequently. Add the orange rind and juice, marmalade, red pepper and plenty of seasonings and heat to melt the marmalade, then pour over the pheasant and cover tightly.

Cook in a moderate oven (160°C/325°F, Gas Mark 3) for about 1^1/2 hours until tender. Serve the pheasant on a warm dish surrounded with the onions and chestnuts. Strain the sauce and serve separately.

A mixture of freshly chopped mixed herbs may be sprinkled overall, if liked.
SERVES 3-4

Note: the chestnuts used for this recipe may be well-drained canned whole chestnuts, freshly boiled and peeled chestnuts or reconstituted dried ones.

PHEASANT PULAO

This recipe is loosely based on an Indian favourite.

1 large onion, peeled and sliced
1-2 cloves garlic, crushed
3 tablespoons oil
1 oven ready pheasant
750 ml/1^1/4 pints stock or water
6 cardamom seeds
6 whole peppercorns
6 whole cloves
1 level teaspoon coriander seeds
^{1}/2 level teaspoon salt
225g/8oz long grain rice
1 green or red pepper, deseeded and sliced
100g/4oz walnut pieces
2-3 dessert apples or peaches or 4-6 plums, cored and sliced
Freshly chopped parsley

Fry the onion and garlic in the oil in a large heavy based saucepan until just soft. Cut the flesh from the carcase of the pheasant and cut into cubes; then add to the pan and continue until the pheasant is lightly browned and completely sealed. Add the stock or water, spices and salt and bring up to the boil. Cover and simmer for about 30 minutes or until almost tender. Add the rice to the pan followed by the pepper, walnuts and apples. Cover the pan and simmer gently until all the liquid has been absorbed – about 25 minutes. If the rice is still a little firm, add a little extra boiling liquid and continue until this is absorbed.

Give the pulao a gentle stir and turn out onto a warmed serving dish; the pheasant should remain on top of the rice. Serve sprinkled liberally with chopped parsley.
SERVES 4-6

PHEASANT PULAO

Pheasant recipes

PHEASANT WITH CELERY

Pheasant poached in a herb-flavoured sauce.

  1 large pheasant, oven ready
  2 heads celery, trimmed and tied
  with string
  2 large carrots, peeled and chopped
  2 onions, peeled and chopped
  1 bay leaf
  1 level teaspoon each dried
  marjoram and parsley
  $1/2$ level teaspoon dried thyme
  2 x 300ml/10 fl oz cans condensed
  consommé
  300 ml/$1/2$ pint wine or water (or a
  mixture)
  Salt and black pepper
  175g/6oz butter
  50g/2oz flour
  4 slices bread (brown or white)
  2 tablespoons double cream
  To garnish:
  Parsley or watercress

Place the heads of celery, carrots, onions and herbs in a large saucepan and add the consommé and wine and/or water. Bring to the boil and simmer for 30 minutes. Season the mixture and add the pheasant and continue to simmer for 30-40 minutes, depending on the size of the bird, until tender. Remove the pheasant and celery and keep warm. Strain the cooking liquor and boil until reduced to 550 ml/ barely a pint. Melt 50g/2oz of the butter in a pan, stir in the flour and cook for a minute or so. Gradually add the cooking liquor and bring up to the boil until thickened. Season to taste and simmer for a couple of minutes.

Meanwhile fry the bread (cut into triangles) in about 50g/2oz of the remaining butter until crisp and golden. Gradually whisk the remaining butter into the sauce, followed by the cream.

Place the pheasant on a serving dish with the celery cut into approx 5cm/2in lengths around it and pour the sauce over, putting the remainder in a separate jug. Garnish with fried bread triangles and parsley or watercress.
SERVES 4

FRICASSEE OF PHEASANT

Pheasant flavoured with wine, mushrooms, cream and capers.

  1-2 mature pheasants (depending
  on size), jointed
  1 large onion, peeled and chopped
  2 rashers bacon, derinded and
  chopped
  2 carrots, peeled and chopped
  450ml/$3/4$ pint stock or water
  150ml/$1/4$ pint dry white wine
  1 tablespoon lemon juice
  Bouquet garni or 2 bay leaves
  50g/2oz butter or margarine
  40g/$11/2$oz flour
  1 level tablespoon capers
  100g/4oz button mushrooms,
  quartered
  3-4 tablespoons double cream
  1 egg yolk (optional)
  To garnish:
  Freshly chopped parsley
  8 crescents fried bread

Place the pieces of pheasant in a large saucepan with the onion, bacon, carrot, stock, wine, lemon juice, bouquet garni or bay leaves and bring slowly up to the boil. Remove the scum from the surface, cover and simmer gently for about 45 minutes or until quite tender. Remove the pheasant to a dish and keep warm.

PHEASANT
WITH CELERY

FRICASSEE OF
PHEASANT

Strain the cooking liquor and reserve 550 ml/barely a pint. Melt the butter in a pan, stir in the flour and cook for a minute or so. Gradually add the cooking liquor and bring to the boil. Add capers and mushrooms and simmer for 2-3 minutes. Season to taste. Blend the cream and egg yolk together and gradually whisk into the sauce. Reheat gently and pour over the pheasant. Serve with chopped parsley and crescents of fried bread.
SERVES 4

PHEASANT VERONIQUE

Grapes blend well with game and make this a good dish for entertaining.

1 large pheasant or 2 small
pheasants, oven ready, quartered
Salt and pepper
25g/1oz butter or margarine
2 tablespoons oil
2 tablespoons brandy or calvados
150ml/1/4 pint dry white wine
150ml/1/4 pint stock
1 tablespoon lemon juice
1/4 level teaspoon ground coriander
175g/6oz seedless green grapes
4-6 tablespoons double cream
1 level teaspoon cornflour
To garnish:
Chopped parsley

Halve each quarter of pheasant and season well. Heat the butter and oil in a pan and fry the pieces of pheasant gently for about 10 minutes until well browned and partly cooked. Strain off the excess fat from the pan. Pour the brandy over the pheasant and ignite, then add the wine, stock and lemon juice to the pan. Bring to the boil, cover and simmer for 15 minutes until the pheasant is tender. Season well

with salt, pepper and coriander and add the grapes. Simmer for 3-4 minutes. Blend the cream with the cornflour and add to the pan. Bring slowly to the boil until just thickened. Serve sprinkled with parsley and with baked jacket potatoes.
SERVES 4

PHEASANT BREASTS IN MUSTARD CREAM SAUCE

A quick and delicious way of serving pheasant, but the birds must be young for pan frying.

4 pheasant breasts, wings attached
Salt and pepper
40g/11/2 oz butter or margarine
1 tablespoon oil
2-3 tablespoons brandy
11/2-2 level tablespoons tarragon
and thyme mustard
150 ml/1/4 pint single cream
To garnish:
Fresh tarragon or parsley

Remove the skin from the pheasant portions and season lightly with salt and pepper, if liked. Melt the butter and oil in a pan and add the pieces of pheasant. Cook gently for about 15 minutes, turning at least twice until golden brown and just cooked through. Pour the brandy over the pheasant, and ignite. Remove the pieces to a serving dish; keep warm.
Stir the mustard into the pan juices, remove from the heat and when smooth, stir in the cream until blended. Reheat gently, adjust the seasonings and spoon back over the pheasant. Garnish with fresh tarragon or parsley and serve with boiled new potatoes and broccoli or a salad.
SERVES 4

PHEASANT VERONIQUE

PHEASANT BREASTS IN MUSTARD CREAM SAUCE

Pheasant recipes

PHEASANT BREASTS CHAUDFROID

This makes an attractive addition to a buffet lunch table.

1 brace pheasants, roasted
150ml/¹/4 pint liquid aspic jelly
150ml/¹/4 pint Bechamel or white
sauce or thick mayonnaise
To garnish:
Stuffed olives and cucumber skin

Carefully remove the breasts from the pheasants and strip off the skin. Wipe the flesh so it is dry, stand on a plate or baking tin and chill. Leave the aspic until it is cold and beginning to thicken then mix half of it evenly through the sauce or mayonnaise. Leave until thick but not set then spoon evenly over the pheasant. Chill until set.

Repeat if necessary with a second coat (the chaudfroid may be melted down again gently). Make a decoration on each piece of pheasant using slices of olive and strips of cucumber skin to represent flowers and leaves. Keep the remaining aspic just liquid and spoon carefully over the decoration and chaudfroid to cover evenly, but without disturbing. Chill again and then serve with salads.
SERVES 4

Note: not suitable to freeze.

PHEASANT BREASTS CHAUDFROID
(pictured right)

PHEASANT BREASTS WITH SPINACH IN FILO PASTRY

These parcels can be prepared earlier in the day, covered until ready to cook, then brushed again with butter.

2 oven-ready pheasants
Salt and pepper
75g/3oz butter or margarine
1 tablespoon oil
1 small onion, peeled and finely chopped
1 clove garlic, crushed
100g/4oz frozen spinach, thawed and chopped, or cooked fresh spinach, chopped
100g/4oz cottage cheese
1 level tablespoon grated Parmesan cheese
1 egg, beaten
8 sheets filo pastry

Remove the breasts carefully from the pheasants and season well.

Melt 25g/1oz butter and the oil in a pan and fry the breasts until golden brown all over and partly cooked; cool. Discard all but 1 tablespoon fat from the pan and fry the onion and garlic until soft.

Turn into a bowl and mix with the spinach, cottage and Parmesan cheeses, seasonings and egg. Cool. Melt the remaining butter. Put four sheets of filo pastry on a flat surface and brush with butter.

Spread each with a quarter of the spinach mixture keeping it to one end of the pastry and in from the edges. Stand a pheasant breast on each and wrap up in the pastry to enclose.

Brush 4 more sheets of pastry with butter and use to overwrap the parcels to give a thicker layer. Stand the parcels on a greased baking sheet and brush all over with melted butter. Cook in a fairly hot oven (200°C/ 400°F, Gas Mark 6) for 30-35 minutes or until a good golden brown. Serve hot with cranberry sauce. Creamed potatoes and vegetables or a salad make a good accompaniment.
SERVES 4

PHEASANT BREASTS WITH SPINACH IN FILO PASTRY
(pictured below)

Pheasant recipes

STIR FRY PHEASANT WITH GINGER (*pictured on page 11*)

Use the legs from a pheasant where the breasts have already been used or strip the flesh from a whole bird. Traditionally a wok is used for stir fry, but a heavy-based pan is just as good.

4-6 pheasant legs or 1 large pheasant, oven ready
2 tablespoons sesame/vegetable oil
1 large onion, peeled and very thinly sliced
2.5cm/1in piece root ginger, peeled and grated
4 sticks celery, sliced
50g/2oz walnut halves or pecan halves
2 courgettes, trimmed and thinly sliced
2 tablespoons sherry
2 tablespoons light soy sauce
Grated rind and juice of 1 orange
1 level tablespoon brown sugar
Good pinch of ground allspice
Salt and black pepper

Remove all the flesh from the pheasant and cut into narrow strips. Heat half the oil in a wok or heavy-based frying pan and fry the onion and ginger for about 5 minutes. Add the celery and continue for 3-4 minutes; then remove from the pan. Add the rest of the oil to the pan and when hot add the pheasant. Stir fry for about 8 minutes until just cooked then add the walnuts, courgettes, sherry, soy sauce, orange rind and juice , sugar and allspice and cook for 2-3 minutes. Return the onion mixture to the pan, season well and stir fry for a minute or so until piping hot. Serve with boiled rice or Chinese egg noodles.
SERVES 4

FAISAN EN PAPILLOTES

A French way of cooking halved small, young pheasants in paper bags.

2 young pheasants, oven-ready
Butter
Salt and pepper
4 tablespoons Madeira, port or sherry
4 rashers unsmoked bacon derinded
4 sprigs fresh herbs – thyme, rosemary, parsley
4 sheets greaseproof paper approx 50 x 25cm/20 x 10in

Stand the pheasants in a roasting tin, brush with 25-40g/1-1^1/2oz melted butter and season lightly. Lay the birds on their sides and cook in a hot oven (220°C/425°F, Gas Mark 7) for 10 minutes. Turn onto their other sides and continue for 10-15 minutes.

To prepare the papillotes, fold each piece of greaseproof paper in half to give a square then cut into a rough heart shape with the point of the heart at the open end. Open out the paper and grease liberally with butter. Remove pheasants from the oven and split each in half. Place one portion on one half of each piece of paper and season well. Spoon the Madeira over the pheasant, cover with bacon and a sprig of herbs and any juices from the roasting tin. Fold over the edges, twist the paper together so no juice can escape, or use paper clips or staples.

Put them onto baking sheets and cook in a moderately hot oven (190°C/375°F, Gas Mark 5) for 15-20 minutes. Serve on hot plates so each guest can open his own parcel of pheasant.
SERVES 4

Note: not suitable to freeze.

STIR FRY PHEASANT
WITH GINGER

FAISAN EN
PAPILLOTES

PHEASANT WITH LIME AND LEMON (*pictured on page 10*)

The pheasant for this recipe needs to be marinated for two days.

1 large or 2 small pheasants, oven ready
Finely grated rind and juice of 2 limes and 2 lemons
3-4 strands saffron or ½ level teaspoon ground turmeric
25g/1oz butter or margarine
2 tablespoons oil
2 tablespoons clear honey
1 level teaspoon dried thyme or 2 level teaspoons freshly chopped thyme
2 level teaspoons dried mint or 2 level tablespoons freshly chopped mint
12 black olives
Salt and black pepper
25g/1oz flaked almonds, toasted

Wipe the pheasant and cut into quarters or eighths depending on size. Place in a shallow container and prick all over. Mix the grated fruit rinds with the juices, pour over the pheasant and rub it well into it. Cover and marinate in the refrigerator for 2 days turning it over, if possible twice a day.

When ready to cook put the saffron or turmeric into 4 tablespoons boiling water and leave for 5 minutes. Melt the butter and oil in a large pan and fry the drained pheasant pieces slowly in the fat until a light golden brown and almost cooked. Add the saffron liquid, honey, remaining marinade, the thyme, half the mint and seasonings. Bring to the boil, cover and simmer gently for about 30 minutes. Add the olives and continue for 5-10 minutes until tender, basting from time to time. Sprinkle with the remaining mint or parsley and almonds, and serve with sautéed potatoes and a green vegetable. SERVES 4

PHEASANT BREASTS IN ASPARAGUS AND ASPIC

Take the breasts from a roasted bird, which must not be overcooked or they will become dry as they get cold.

1 brace pheasants, roasted
450ml/¾ pint liquid aspic jelly (1 packet)
1 can asparagus spears, drained or 12-16 fresh asparagus spears, cooked
To garnish
Lemon slices

Remove the breasts carefully from the pheasants and discard the skin. Wipe the flesh so it is dry and put on a plate or baking tray; chill. Make up the aspic jelly and leave until cold.

Pour half into a bowl and chill until beginning to thicken. Brush over the pheasant breasts and return to the refrigerator; leave the aspic out. Repeat brushing with aspic twice more. Trim the asparagus to fit the pieces of pheasant, dip 4 or 8 spears into the liquid aspic and lay on the breasts.

Brush the whole thing with aspic and chill. Give a further one or two coats of aspic and then chill again along with the remainder of the aspic.

To serve, chop the surplus set aspic jelly. Place the breasts on a serving dish and surround with the chopped aspic, the remaining asparagus and a few twists of lemon. SERVES 4

PHEASANT WITH LIME AND LEMON

PHEASANT BREASTS IN ASPARAGUS AND ASPIC

PARTRIDGE
ENGLISH AND FRENCH

THERE are two varieties of partridge available in this country – the red-legged or French partridge and the grey or English partridge. The larger of the two is the red-legged, so named mainly because of its red legs, while the smaller grey partridge is often preferred for flavour.

The grey's legs are olive-coloured and the beak tends to be supple, softer and darker in colour in the young birds. In both varieties the primary feathers are pointed in young birds, but they become rounded with age.

Partridges are at their best in October and November and one bird will usually serve only one person, though if large they may be split to make two small portions. They should be hung for 4-8 days depending of course on weather conditions and personal taste; but as with all game they do need to be hung.

Young birds are best simply roasted, but they are also excellent spatchcooked and grilled or pan fried. Older birds are better with longer, slower methods of cooking.

BASIC ROAST PARTRIDGE

These birds are usually roasted unstuffed, sometimes with the liver returned to the body cavity, but they can be filled with a non-meat type of stuffing such as mushroom (see over).

2-4 partridges, oven ready
Salt and pepper
Melted dripping, butter or oil
Streaky bacon rashers
To serve:
Lemon wedges
Watercress
Bread sauce and/or fried crumbs
Game chips or matchstick potatoes

Wipe the birds inside and out and replace the liver in the cavity, or add a knob of butter; or stuff loosely with the mushroom stuffing and secure or sew up loosely.

Truss the birds, place in a roasting tin and pour melted fat over them. Season lightly and if liked (or if available) lay a vine leaf over the breast of each; then cover with the streaky bacon rashers. Cook in a hot oven (220°C/425°F, Gas Mark 7) for 25-45 minutes depending on size.

Baste several times during cooking and remove the bacon and vine leaf before serving. Remove the trussing string and serve on a warmed dish garnished with watercress and lemon wedges and with game chips or matchstick potatoes if liked. Serve bread sauce and/or fried crumbs with the partridges with a thin gravy made using the pan juices with the excess fat spooned off.
SERVES 2-4

See over for mushroom stuffing

BASIC ROAST PARTRIDGE

PARTRIDGE WITH GRAPES AND ORANGE SAUCE
(pictured opposite, recipe on page 28)

CREAMED PARTRIDGE
(pictured below, recipe on page 29)

Partridge recipes

Mushroom Stuffing:
1 small onion, peeled and chopped
25g/1oz butter or margarine
75g/3oz button mushrooms, chopped
1 pickled walnut, chopped
Salt and pepper
50g/2oz fresh breadcrumbs (brown or white)
1/2 level teaspoon dried thyme
Beaten egg to bind

Fry the onion in the melted fat until soft. Add the mushrooms and continue for a minute or so. Remove from the heat and stir in all the other ingredients adding sufficient beaten egg to bind. When cold use to stuff the cavities of the birds.

CASSEROLE OF PARTRIDGE

Tangy apples give a bite to this dish, along with ham, cider and cream.

4 partridges, oven ready
Salt and black pepper
25g/1oz butter or margarine
2 tablespoons oil
1 onion, peeled and chopped
100g/4oz cooked ham, chopped
1 cooking apple, peeled, cored and sliced
1 clove garlic, crushed
1 bay leaf
4 tablespoons stock or cider
150ml/1/4 pint single cream
2 tablespoons brandy
To garnish:
Watercress

Truss the birds lightly and season if liked. Melt the butter and oil in a pan and fry the partridges until browned all over. Remove from the pan. Add the onion to the pan and fry for a few minutes until soft, then add the ham, apple and garlic and continue for a few minutes more. Turn into a casserole and place the partridges on top. Add the bay leaf and pour on the stock or cider. Season and cover the casserole. Cook in a moderate oven (160°C/325°F, Gas Mark 3) for 1/2 hour. Discard the bay leaf, add the cream to the casserole and pour the brandy over the birds. Cover again and return to the oven for 1/2 hour.

Serve the partridges on a serving dish surrounded by the ham mixture and with the juices in a sauce boat. Garnish with watercress.
SERVES 4

PARTRIDGE WITH GRAPES AND ORANGE SAUCE (*pictured on page 26*)

Grapes and orange blend well with the taste and texture of partridges.

4 partridges, oven ready
50g/2oz butter or margarine
1 orange, quartered
Salt and pepper
1-2 tablespoons oil
4 rounds of toast or fried bread
Grated rind and juice of 1 orange
250ml/8 fl oz stock
1 level teaspoon cornflour
100g/4oz green grapes, halved and depipped (or left whole if seedless)
To garnish:
Orange quarters
Small bunches of green and black grapes
Watercress or fresh herbs

Wipe the partridges and put a knob of butter and a piece of orange in the cavity of each bird. Stand in a roasting tin; rub the remaining butter over the birds. Season lightly, if liked. Add the oil to the pan and cook in a hot oven (220°C/425°F, Gas Mark 7) for 35-45 minutes, basting several times, or until tender and just cooked through.

Remove to a serving dish standing each partridge on a round of toast; keep warm. Spoon off excess fat from the pan juices, add the grated rind and juice of the orange, stock and seasonings and bring to the boil, stirring continuously. Blend the cornflour in a little cold water and add to the pan. Bring back to boil and add the grapes. Simmer for 3-4 minutes then serve with a little spooned over each birds and the remainder in a sauce boat. Garnish with orange quarters, grapes and watercress or fresh herbs.
SERVES 4

BOILED PARTRIDGE WITH VINE LEAVES

Vine leaves are easily obtainable from delicatessens and European stores if you can't find fresh ones.

4 partridges, oven ready
Salt and pepper
8 rashers streaky bacon, derinded
Approx 16-20 vine leaves
Stock
Juice of 1 lemon
To garnish:
Salads

Trim the partridges, if necessary and season inside and out. Cover completely with first bacon rashers and then vine leaves, tying in place with cotton or fine string. Put into a saucepan just large enough to hold the birds and cover with seasoned stock to which the lemon juice has been added. Bring to the boil, cover and simmer gently for about 40 minutes or until tender. Remove from the stock and plunge each bird immediately into iced water and leave until just cold. Drain very thoroughly and chill.

Serve with a mixed green salad of different lettuces and a potato salad by mixing diced cooked potatoes with sliced hard-boiled eggs, chives and parsley in mayonnaise and yoghurt.
SERVES 4

CREAMED PARTRIDGE

(pictured on page 27)

Whole birds pan fried in butter with herbs, bacon, mushrooms and cream.

4 partridges, oven ready
Salt and pepper
100g/4oz butter
4 rounds toast
2-3 tablespoons each of finely chopped onion and lean raw bacon
1 level tablespoon freshly chopped mixed herbs
100g/4oz button mushrooms, sliced
150ml/1/4 pint double cream
To garnish:
Watercress

Wipe the partridges inside and out and season all with salt and pepper. Melt the butter in a large pan and fry the birds all over gently until evenly browned. Cover the pan and continue to cook slowly for about 3 minutes, turning the birds once or twice until tender. Remove to a serving dish, standing each on a round of toast and keep warm. Add the onion and bacon to the pan and fry gently for a few minutes more. Add the cream and heat gently to just below boiling point. Season to taste and spoon over the partridges. Garnish with watercress.
SERVES 4

BOILED PARTRIDGE WITH VINE LEAVES

CREAMED PARTRIDGE

Partridge recipes

PARTRIDGE IN MADEIRA

The partridges adopt the flavour of Madeira as they poach in the sauce.

450ml/^{3}/4 pint stock
1 onion, peeled and chopped
2 carrots, peeled and chopped
1 bay leaf
1 clove garlic, crushed
150ml/^{1}/4 pint Madeira or Marsala
4 partridges, oven ready
Salt and pepper
Little seasoned flour
2 tablespoons oil
4 round fried bread or toast
Tomato sauce:
450g/1lb tomatoes, peeled
2 tablespoons oil
1 clove garlic, crushed
1 level tablespoon freshly chopped parsley
To garnish:
Parsley

Put the stock, onion, carrots, bay leaf and garlic into a saucepan, bring to the boil, cover and simmer for 15 minutes then add the Madeira.

Meanwhile coat the partridges in seasoned flour and fry slowly to brown all over in the heated oil – about 10-15 minutes. Add the partridges to the stock, season well, cover and simmer gently for about ^{3}/4 hour, turning over several times or until tender.

While they are cooking make the tomato sauce; quarter the tomatoes, remove the seeds and place in a pan with the oil, garlic and seasonings. Cover and cook gently for about 20 minutes or until well broken down and thick, stirring occasionally. Remove partridges to a warm serving dish and stand on the fried rounds of bread; keep warm. Strain the cooking liquor and boil hard until reduced to about 150 ml/^{1}/4 pint. Add the tomato mixture and parsley and reheat. Adjust the seasonings and serve in a sauce boat with the partridges garnished with parsley.
SERVES 4

Note: Young pigeons and grouse may also be cooked in this way but increase the cooking time by about 20 minutes.

MARINATED PARTRIDGE

A spicy marinade gives both flavour and succulence to the partridges.

4 partridges, oven ready and halved
Salt and pepper
Marinade:
1-2 cloves garlic, crushed
Grated rind of 1 lemon
4 tablespoons walnut oil
2 tablespoons lemon juice
4 tablespoons orange juice
1 teaspoon Angostura bitters
Salt and pepper
2 tablespoons melted butter
50g/2oz shelled walnuts, chopped
4-6 spring onions, thinly sliced
Shredded iceburg lettuce
To garnish:
Orange wedges

Season the pieces of partridge lightly and place in a shallow container in a single layer. Combine the garlic, lemon rind, oil, lemon and orange juice, bitters and seasonings. Pour over the partridges, cover and leave to marinate in a cool place for at least 6 hours, turning at least twice so the marinade reaches all parts of the birds. Drain and place in a foil lined

PARTRIDGE IN MADEIRA

MARINATED PARTRIDGE

grill pan and brush with melted butter. Cook under a moderate heat for about 5 minutes each side, then turn skin side upwards again and spoon a little marinade over and cook for a further 5-10 minutes until cooked through. Heat the marinade gently, add the chopped walnuts, onions and seasonings and juices from the grill pan.

Serve the partridges on a bed of shredded lettuce with the sauce spooned over, garnished with orange wedges.
SERVES 4

Note: the partridges may be put into a roasting tin, skin side upwards, with the butter and marinade poured over and cooked in a hot oven (200°C/400°F, Gas Mark 6) for 20-30 minutes.

CRUNCHY TOPPED PARTRIDGE

A crispy topping is added to the birds which are served with a lime and parsley sauce.

4 partridges, oven ready
1 lime or small lemon, quartered
50g/2oz butter or margarine
1 tablespoon oil
Salt and pepper
6-8 level tablespoons dry packet parsley and thyme stuffing mix
Sauce:
2 tablespoons fat from the cooking juices
1 level tablespoon flour
150 ml/1/4 pint dry white wine
150 ml/1/4 pint stock
Grated rind of 1 lemon
2 level tablespoons freshly chopped parsley
To garnish:
Twists or slices of lime

Place a quarter of lime or lemon in the cavity of each partridge and rub all over with softened butter. Season lightly and stand in a roasting tin.

Pour the oil overall and cook in a hot oven (220°C/425°F, Gas Mark 7) for 30 minutes basting once. Baste again and spoon the stuffing mix over the birds. Return to the oven for 15-25 minutes until cooked through and the topping is crispy.

Meanwhile make the sauce: transfer 2 tablespoons fat from the roasting pan to a saucepan, stir in the flour and cook for a minute or so. Gradually add the wine and stock and bring to the boil, stirring all the time. Stir in the lime rind and parsley, season to taste and simmer for a minute or so. Serve the partridges garnished with twists of lime with the sauce and with baked jacket potatoes and vegetables such as baby carrots and broccoli or courgettes.
SERVES 4

CRUNCHY TOPPED PARTRIDGE
(pictured below)

Partridge recipes

PARTRIDGE WITH JUNIPER

The pleasant flavour and aroma of juniper berries adds greatly to this dish.

4 partridges, oven ready
Salt and pepper
8 rashers streaky bacon
1 small onion, peeled and quartered
16 juniper berries, crushed
40g/1^1/2 oz butter or margarine
2 tablespoons oil
4-6 tablespoons brandy
4 small rounds toast
150 ml/^{1}/4 pint stock
To garnish:
spring onion tassles

Season the birds lightly, lay the bacon over the breasts and put a piece of onion and 2 crushed juniper berries in the cavity of each. Rub with the fat and stand in a roasting tin. Pour oil overall and cook in a hot oven (220°C/425°F, Gas Mark 7) for 30 minutes, basting twice. Pour the brandy over the birds and ignite, add the remaining juniper berries to the pan and return to the oven for 5-10 minutes. Remove the birds to a serving dish and stand each on a round of toast. Keep warm. Spoon off excess fat from the pan juices, add the stock and bring to the boil. Boil hard for a minute or so until slightly glazed and well reduced. Adjust seasonings and strain the sauce. Either spoon over the partridges or serve in a sauce boat.

Garnish with spring onion tassles. Serve with a finely shredded white cabbage cooked in milk and Lyonnaise potatoes (cubes or slices of potato fried with sliced onions).
SERVES 4

SPATCHCOCKED PARTRIDGE

This is an old English method of cooking gamebirds, by splitting down the back, laying them flat and grilling under heat or over charcoal. They can be brushed with a variety of ingredients before cooking. It is an ideal way to barbecue game, and you can use frozen birds provided they are fully thawed before you cut them.

4 partridges, oven ready
Salt and black pepper
2 cloves garlic, crushed
2 level tablespoons French mustard
2 level teaspoons freshly chopped tarragon or 1 level teaspoon dried tarragon
Oil
To garnish:
Watercress sprigs
Lemon wedges

Cut each bird carefully along one side of the backbone, press the bird open flat, cracking any bones as necessary. Hold the bird flat by inserting two skewers (wooden or metal) diagonally across it. Rub the birds all over with salt and pepper and then with garlic and then spread with mustard. Sprinkle with tarragon (and a few drops of oil if liked) and place on a grill rack.

Cook under a moderate grill for about 10 minutes each side, adding a little more oil when you turn them, until just cooked through and crisp. Serve garnished with watercress and lemon wedges.

To cook on a barbecue, simply cook for 10-15 minutes, turning several times, depending on the heat of the barbecue, until tender.
SERVES 4

PARTRIDGE WITH JUNIPER

SPATCHCOCKED PARTRIDGE

GRILLED PARTRIDGE WITH WATERCRESS SAUCE

For each person you will need a whole partridge which is split in half and grilled. This is a very quick and delicious way of cooking young partridges.

4 young partridges, oven ready
40g/1¹/₂ oz butter, melted
Salt and pepper
About 8 level tablespoons
fresh breadcrumbs,
brown or white
To garnish:
Watercress
Lemon slices
Gherkin fans
Watercress Sauce:
1 bunch watercress, trimmed
1-2 level tablespoons snipped
chives
150ml/¹/₄ pint natural yogurt or
fromage frais
4 tablespoons thick mayonnaise

Split the partridges in two along the backbone and flatten each piece slightly. Brush with melted butter, stand on a lined grill for 4-5 minutes each side. Brush again liberally with butter with the skin side upwards and sprinkle with the breadcrumbs. Replace under the grill for about 5 minutes or until the crumbs are golden brown and the partridges just cooked through – take care not to over cook.

For the sauce, combine all the ingredients, season to taste and put into a bowl. Arrange the partridges on a serving dish and garnish with watercress, lemon slices and gherkin fans and serve with the sauce.
SERVES 4

PAN FRIED PARTRIDGE WITH PEARS

A quick way to deal with young birds which will grace any table.

2 young partridges, oven ready
Salt and pepper
40g/1¹/₂ oz butter or margarine
2 tablespoons oil
1 small onion, peeled and very
finely chopped
2 firm pears, peeled, cored and
thickly sliced
4 whole cloves
Grated rind of ¹/₂ orange
Juice of 2 oranges
150ml/¹/₄ pint white wine
150ml/¹/₄ pint stock
3-4 tablespoons cream or
fromage frais
To garnish:
Watercress
Wedges of orange

Cut the birds completely in half and season lightly. Heat the butter and oil in a frying pan, add the pieces of partridge and fry for about 10 minutes, turning several times until well browned all over and partly cooked through. Add the onion and continue for a minute or so then add the pears, cloves, orange rind and juice, wine and stock. Bring to the boil, spoon the sauce over the partridges and then cover and simmer gently for about 20 minutes until tender. Remove partridges and pears and keep warm.

Boil the pan juices until reduced to 4-5 tablespoons, then stir in the cream or fromage frais, reheat gently and adjust seasonings. Spoon the sauce over the partridges and serve with watercress and orange wedges.
SERVES 2

GRILLED PARTRIDGE WITH WATERCRESS SAUCE

PAN FRIED PARTRIDGE WITH PEARS

PIGEON
TASTY AND VERSATILE

THE WILD woodpigeon, the feral pigeon and the tame pigeon may be eaten, but it is the woodpigeon which tastes most like game, though strictly it is not classed as game. Huge numbers of woodpigeon are shot as they do tremendous damage to farm and garden crops. Fortunately the birds taste good – no small wonder when they feed voraciously and consistently on corn, peas, cabbage and many other nutritious foods. Consequently the birds are easy to obtain and cheap, though supermarket prices are often inflated.

A young bird is, of course, the best for cooking. It is best to cook pigeon fresh, though some people like to hang them for a day or so, but the crops should be removed first, and certainly do not allow them to hang for long. They are very easy to pluck but if you are presented with a large number it is often better to speed the proceedings and cut along the breastbone with a sharp knife and peel off the skin and feathers together so that the bird can be lifted out.

Draw as usual but leave the legs and feet on; these should be scalded and scraped. Alternatively, as most of the meat is on the breast, simply skin the breast and remove the two 'steaks' with a sharp knife if your recipe does not stipulate whole birds.

Pigeon will freeze well and are widely available from many supermarkets, game and farm shops. Fresh birds can be obtained from fishmongers, butchers and poulterers as well as game merchants.

Pigeon are best roasted only if young; otherwise casserole or braise or cook them using a longer, slower method. If to be used for a pie they are best pre-cooked. With whole birds allow one per person but allow more if using only the breasts.

Cooked pigeon dishes may be frozen for up to 2 months.

**PIGEON
BOULANGERE**
*(pictured opposite,
recipe on page 37)*

**PIGEON CASSEROLE
WITH DUMPLINGS**
*(pictured left,
recipe on page 38)*

Pigeon recipes

BASIC ROAST PIGEON

The addition of a piece of apple or orange helps keep the meat nice and moist in this simple recipe.

4 pigeons, oven ready
1 dessert apple or small orange, quartered
Streaky bacon rashers
Salt and pepper
Oil or dripping

Wipe the birds all over and insert a quarter of apple or orange in the cavity of each one. This gives flavour and helps to keep the flesh moist.

Lay the bacon over the breast of the birds and stand in a roasting tin. Season and cover liberally with oil or dripping. Cook in a fairly hot oven (200°C/400°F, Gas Mark 6) for about 30 minutes, basting once or twice, or until well browned and tender. Take care not to overcook.

Serve each bird on a crouton of fried bread or toast, and garnish with watercress. Serve with a gravy made using the pan juices and flavoured with wine if liked; and with cranberry sauce or jelly.

Pigeon may also be stuffed before cooking, which also helps to keep them moist.

For the stuffing, fry 2 chopped pigeon livers in 1 tablespoon oil with 2 chopped rashers of bacon. Mix with 1 level tablespoon each chopped onion and freshly chopped parsley, $1/2$ level teaspoon grated lemon rind, 6-8 tablespoons fresh breadcrumbs, salt, pepper and a pinch of ground nutmeg and bind together with beaten egg.

Allow an extra 7-10 minutes cooking time if stuffing the birds.

PIGEON LOUISETTE

Whole pigeons casseroled in Marsala with mushrooms, juniper berries and cream.

4 plump pigeons, oven ready
1 small orange, quartered
Salt and pepper
8 rashers streaky bacon, derinded
1 tablespoon oil
25g/1oz butter or margarine
1 large onion, peeled and chopped
1 level tablespoon flour
6-8 tablespoons Marsala or red wine
300ml/$1/2$ pint stock
100g/4oz button mushrooms, thickly sliced
6 juniper berries, crushed
3-4 tablespoons cream (optional)

Place a piece of orange in the cavity of each pigeon and season lightly. Lay 2 rashers bacon over each bird and secure with cotton or fine string.

Heat the oil and fat in a pan and fry the pigeons until browned all over. Transfer to an ovenproof casserole. Fry the onion in the same fat until beginning to brown, then stir in the flour and cook for 1 minute.

Gradually add the Marsala or wine and stock and bring up to the boil, stirring frequently. Add the mushrooms and juniper berries and season well. Pour over the pigeons, cover tightly and cook in a moderate oven (180°C/350°F, Gas Mark 4) for 1-1$1/2$ hours until tender.

Adjust seasonings and stir in the cream, if used. Remove string from the birds and serve with freshly boiled rice or creamed potatoes and a green vegetable.
SERVES 4

BASIC ROAST PIGEON

PIGEON LOUISETTE

PIGEON SUPREME WITH MADEIRA

A simple pan fried recipe using just the breasts of the birds which is particularly good; but the pigeons must be young.

8 pigeon breasts
Salt and pepper
40g/1¹/₂oz butter or margarine
100ml/4fl oz orange juice (not squash)
3 tablespoons stock
3-4 tablespoons Madeira (or sherry)
Grated rind of 2 oranges
50g/2oz liver pâté
¹/₂ - 1 level teaspoon arrowroot
To garnish:
Stuffed olives and parsley

Skin the pigeon breasts and season lightly. Melt the fat in a pan and add the breasts. Cook gently until lightly coloured all over then add the orange juice, stock, Madeira, half the orange rind and a little seasoning.

Bring slowly to the boil, cover and simmer gently for about 20 minutes, turning once.

Beat the pâté until smooth and add a touch of Madeira or stock to give a softish consistency. Place the pigeon breasts on a serving dish and top each with a spoonful of the soft pâté; keep warm.

Blend the arrowroot with a little cold water and add to the pan juices. Bring back to the boil until very slightly thickened. Adjust the seasonings and spoon over and around the pieces of pigeon.

Sprinkle with the remaining orange rind and garnish with parsley and stuffed olives.
SERVES 4

PIGEON BOULANGERE

(pictured on page 34)
This is a good way of serving most types of game, and pigeon are no exception. Try it also for chicken, guinea fowl and joints of lamb.

900g/2lb potatoes, peeled and sliced
2 onions, peeled and sliced
2 cloves garlic, crushed
4 pigeons, oven ready
8 rashers streaky bacon
1 lemon, quartered
2 tablespoons oil
Salt and pepper
Few sprigs of fresh rosemary or a little dried rosemary
300ml/¹/₂ pint stock

Layer the potatoes, onions and garlic in a greased roasting tin or large shallowish ovenproof dish and make dips in it for the pigeons.

Wrap the bacon around the birds securing with string, if necessary. Insert a quarter of lemon in the cavity of each bird.

Heat the oil in a pan and fry the birds until browned all over. Place on top of the potatoes, pressing into them as much as possible.

Season well and put the rosemary around them. Bring the stock to the boil and season well. Pour over the potatoes and cover the whole container with foil, very tightly. Cook in a fairly hot oven (200°C/400°F, Gas Mark 6) for about 1¹/₂ hours.

Remove the foil and return to the oven to brown up for about 10 minutes. Serve from the cooking dish garnished with parsley or watercress, if liked.
SERVES 4

PIGEON SUPREME WITH MADEIRA

PIGEON BOULANGERE

Pigeon recipes

SOUSED PIGEON

This recipe takes several days to complete but the effort is worthwhile.

4 pigeons, oven ready
3 tablespoons oil
1 onion, peeled and very thinly sliced
2-3 cloves garlic, crushed
2 level tablespoons salt
18 black peppercorns
2 sprigs fresh rosemary
2 bay leaves (preferably fresh)
6 cardamom seeds, opened (optional)
1 level teaspoon ground allspice
2 level tablespoons dark, soft brown sugar
300ml/$\frac{1}{2}$ pint red wine
300ml/$\frac{1}{2}$ pint white wine vinegar
600ml/1 pint water

SOUSED PIGEON
(pictured below)

PIGEON CASSEROLE WITH DUMPLINGS
(pictured on page 35)

Heat the oil in a pan and fry the pigeons until well browned all over. Transfer to a large casserole. Fry the onion and garlic in the same fat until soft, but not coloured, and add to the pigeons.

Add the salt, peppercorns, rosemary, bay leaves, cardamoms (if used), allspice and sugar. Put the wine, vinegar and water into a pan and bring up to the boil. Pour over the pigeons, cover the casserole and cook in a moderate oven (180°C/350°F, Gas Mark 4) for 45 minutes.

Remove from the oven, turn pigeons so they are resting sideways in the liquid, and leave to cool slowly. When cold, refrigerate for 2-3 days, turning the birds in the liquid twice a day.

To serve, slice all the meat thinly off the birds and put a few onions onto each portion. Do not add any liquid. Offer hot new potatoes or a potato salad and a salad of crisp lettuces and spinach leaves with spring onions and cucumber.
SERVES 4

PIGEON CASSEROLE WITH DUMPLINGS

A rich casserole flavoured with cider and vegetables and topped with dumplings which are added for the last 30 minutes of cooking.

6 rashers streaky bacon, derinded and chopped
25g/1oz butter or margarine
4 plump pigeons, oven ready
50g/2oz flour
300ml/$\frac{1}{2}$ pint dry cider
150ml/$\frac{1}{4}$ pint stock
10 button onions, peeled
2 carrots, peeled and diced
2-3 sticks celery, sliced

1 level teaspoon mixed herbs
Salt and pepper
75g/3oz mushrooms, halved or
quartered
Dumplings:
100g/4oz self-raising flour
50g/2oz shredded suet
1 level tablespoon freshly chopped
parsley
Grated rind and juice of 1 lemon
1 egg, beaten
Water, if necessary
To garnish:
Watercress or parsley

Fry the bacon in the fat until crispy; remove from the pan. Fry the pigeons in the same fat until well browned, then transfer to a casserole. Add the flour to the juices in the pan and cook for a minute or so. Gradually add the cider and stock and bring up to the boil, stirring continuously.

Add the onions, carrots, celery, herbs and seasonings. Pour over the pigeons, sprinkle with the bacon and cover the casserole. Cook in a moderate oven (180°C/350°F, Gas Mark 4) for 1-1¹/2 hours or until the pigeons are nearly tender.

For the dumplings, place all the dry ingredients in a bowl and mix well. Add the lemon juice and egg and a little water if necessary, to give a firm but not too stiff dough. Shape into 8 balls. Stir the mushrooms into the casserole and arrange the dumplings on top. Replace the lid and cook for a further 25-30 minutes.

To serve, remove pigeons and cut in half; place on a serving dish. Arrange the vegetables and dumplings around and pour the sauce overall. Garnish with watercress or parsley.
SERVES 4

POT ROAST PIGEON

Pot roasting is ideal for those birds that may be a little older than you want for roasting or pan frying. This makes a good, hearty dish on a cold day.

4 pigeons, oven ready
2 tablespoons oil
2 cloves garlic, crushed
2 onions, peeled and
sliced
2 large carrots, peeled and
sliced
350g/³/4lb tomatoes, peeled and
quartered
1¹/2 level tablespoons tomato
purée
300ml/¹/2 pint stock or a mixture of
stock and white wine
2 tablespoons capers
100g/4oz mushrooms, trimmed and
quartered
Salt and pepper

Brown the pigeons all over in the heated oil and remove from the pan. Fry the garlic and onions in the same fat for about 5 minutes then add the carrots, tomatoes, tomato purée and stock and bring up to the boil. Add capers and mushrooms and season very well.

Pour into a casserole or baking tin. Arrange the birds on top, burying them as far as possible into the sauce. Cover tightly and cook in a moderate oven (180°C/350°F, Gas Mark 4) for 1¹/4 - 1¹/2 hours until tender.

Remove the lid, baste thoroughly and return to the oven, uncovered for 10 minutes.

Serve with creamed potatoes and vegetables.
SERVES 4

POT ROAST PIGEON

Pigeon recipes

SOMERSET PIGEON CASSEROLE

Add a dash of Calvados to the sauce; or for a more sour sauce use Bramley apples instead of dessert.

4 young plump pigeons, oven ready
1 carrot, peeled and sliced
1 bouquet garni
Little seasoned flour
50g/2oz salt belly pork or streaky bacon
1 large onion, peeled and sliced
1 tablespoon oil or dripping
450g/1lb dessert apples, cored and sliced
1 level teaspoon crushed coriander seeds
1/2 level teaspoon mixed herbs
Salt and pepper
150ml/1/4 pint dry cider
150ml/1/4 pint single cream
2 tablespoons Calvados (optional)
To garnish:
Thick apple slices
Little butter
Parsley

Leave the pigeons whole or cut along each side of breastbone and fillet off the breast wing and leg in one piece to give two portions and a body carcase. Put carcases and any giblets into a saucepan with about 600ml/ 1 pint water, the carrot and bouquet garni and simmer for about 3/4 hour. If leaving the birds whole use 300ml/ 1/2 pint beef or chicken stock. Dry the pigeons and coat in seasoned flour.

Remove rind and gristle from the pork and cut into strips. Fry gently until the fat runs, then add the onion and cook until softened. Add the oil and then fry the pigeons briskly until browned all over. Add the apples,

coriander, herbs and seasonings. Pour in the cider and 300ml/1/2 pint of the strained pigeon stock, or sufficient barely to cover the birds. Cover tightly and cook in a moderate oven (160°C/ 325°F, Gas Mark 3) for 1 1/2 hours or until the pigeons are tender. Mix 3-4 tablespoons of the sauce with the cream, then stir this back into the sauce with the Calvados, if used. Mix thoroughly and adjust the seasonings.

To garnish fry slices of apple gently in butter until lightly browned. Arrange round the birds with parsley.
SERVES 4

PIGEON BREASTS WITH POTATO AND CHIVE GALETTE

Slivers of pigeon served with a delicious potato cake.

6-8 pigeons, breasts only
Salt and pepper
1 clove garlic, crushed
25g/1oz butter or margarine
1 tablespoon oil
3 tablespoons red wine vinegar
150ml/1/4 pint stock
1/4 level teaspoon ground allspice
4-6 tablespoons Greek yoghurt
Potato and Chive Galette:
3 large baking potatoes, scrubbed and baked until soft
50g/2oz butter
2 medium onions, peeled and thinly sliced
Pinch of ground nutmeg or mace
2 level tablespoons freshly chopped chives

Cut the pigeon breasts into thin slices, season with salt and pepper and rub with garlic. Leave to stand for 10-15 minutes.

For the galette, remove the flesh

SOMERSET PIGEON CASSEROLE

PIGEON BREASTS WITH POTATO AND CHIVE GALETTE

from the potatoes and mash thoroughly. Melt half the fat in a pan and fry the onions very gently until golden brown. Add half the remaining butter and when melted add potato, seasonings, nutmeg and 1 tablespoon chives. Mix well as it cooks for a few minutes then level the top making it into a cake. Continue for 4-5 minutes over a gentle heat.

Meanwhile for the pigeon, heat the fat in a frying pan and add the pigeon. Cook until well sealed all over and then add the vinegar and mix thoroughly. Add the stock and bring to the boil. Season well with salt and pepper and add the allspice. Simmer gently for about 10 minutes in a covered pan. Dot the top of the galette with the remaining butter and put under a moderate grill until the top becomes an even golden brown. Slide the galette onto a plate or serve from the pan. Cut into quarters and sprinkle with the rest of the chives. Stir the yoghurt evenly into the pigeon, reheat gently and adjust the seasonings.

Serve on plates with a wedge of the galette and a green vegetable or salad. SERVES 4

PIGEON PIE

The flesh can be removed from the breastbones before adding to the pie, but it is better to leave them intact, if you have a large enough casserole.

> 6 pigeons, breasts only
> 25g/1oz butter or margarine
> 2 tablespoons oil
> 350g/3/4lb stewing steak, cubed
> 16-20 button onions
> 100g/4oz mushrooms, quartered
> 2 slices ham, chopped
> 450ml/3/4 pint red wine
> 4 level tablespoons redcurrant or cranberry jelly
> 2 level teaspoons fresh thyme or 1 level teaspoon dried thyme
> Salt and pepper
> 300ml/1/2 pint stock
> 450g/1lb puff pastry
> beaten egg or milk to glaze

Heat the butter and oil in a pan and fry the pieces of pigeon until well browned all over; transfer to a saucepan. Fry the steak and onions in the same fat until well sealed, add the mushrooms and continue for a few minutes. Add the ham and wine and bring up to the boil, stirring to loosen all the sediment from the pan. Add to the saucepan with the jelly, thyme, plenty of seasoning and the stock and bring back to the boil. Cover and simmer very gently for about 1 1/2 hours or until tender. Turn into a large pie dish with a funnel in the centre and leave to cool. Keep any extra gravy separately.

Roll out the pastry and cut a strip 2.5cm / 1in wide; place this on the dampened rim of the pie dish. Brush with water and position the lid. Trim the edges, flake and crimp; use the trimmings to make leaves to decorate the top of the pie. Glaze with beaten egg, make a hole in the top of the pastry above the funnel and cook in a hot oven (220°C / 425°F, Gas Mark 7) for about 40 minutes. Reduce the temperature to moderate (160°C / 325°F, Gas Mark 3) and continue for about 15 minutes, covering the pie with greaseproof paper when sufficiently browned.

Serve hot with any extra gravy reheated and served in a gravy boat. SERVES 6

PIGEON PIE

GROUSE
A GLORIOUS TRADITION

THERE are several species of these gamebirds in Britain, the best known and most usually referred to as grouse being the red grouse. Red grouse shooting begins on August 12th – the Glorious Twelfth as it is often called – and there is an annual race to see who can get the grouse shot, prepared, cooked and on to the table by fair means (or foul!) first. This often involves aeroplanes, helicopters, fast cars and other modes of transport and the cost to the recipients in a restaurant which proclaims to serve grouse on the Twelfth will be accordingly high!

Grouse are at their best from August until mid-October and require to hang for about a week on average. Young birds should have bright eyes, soft pliable feet and smooth legs, and the breastbone should feel soft and pliable. In older birds this bone becomes hard and the feet and legs become hard and scaly with sharp claws. Only roast young birds, either whole or cut in half, and they may also be halved and grilled if sufficiently tender; keep the mature birds for casserole, pot-roasting, pies, pâtés and terrines.

The black grouse (known collectively as blackgame, the male as the blackcock and the female as the greyhen) is up to twice the size of the red grouse and needs to be well hung before cooking. The flesh tends to be dry except in very young birds so a moist method of cooking is preferable to simple roasting, though any of the grouse recipes can be used for blackcock provided you adjust the cooking times.

Ptarmigan is another member of the grouse family and the smallest member. It turns white in winter and is known by some as white grouse. The flavour is not quite so good as that of the other types of grouse but young birds can be roasted as with red grouse for about 30 minutes or until tender. Older birds should be casseroled with well-flavoured ingredients. If served roasted, both the ptarmigan and blackcock can have the same accompaniments as grouse.

All types of grouse will freeze satisfactorily and those who find difficulty in obtaining them fresh might try larger supermarkets and farm or game shops during the season; and they can be easily obtained frozen out of season from good gamedealers.

GROUSE WITH BLUEBERRIES
(pictured left, recipe on page 45)

POT ROAST OF GROUSE
(pictured below, recipe on page 45)

Grouse recipes

BASIC ROAST GROUSE
Use only young grouse for this dish.

> **2-3 young grouse, oven ready**
> **Salt and pepper**
> **Knob of butter for each bird**
> **2-3 slices or rounds of toast**
> **Melted dripping, butter or oil**
> **Streaky bacon rashers**
> **Little flour**
> *To serve::*
> **Watercress**
> **Matchstick potatoes**
> **Fried breadcrumbs**
> **Bread sauce**

Wipe the birds inside and out, truss lightly, season and put a knob of butter in the cavity of each bird. Stand each on a piece of toast in a roasting tin and pour the melted fat or oil over. Cover the breast of each with rashers of bacon. Cook in a hot oven (220°C/425°F, Gas Mark 7) for 30-45 minutes, baste several times and remove the bacon and dredge the breasts with flour about 10 minutes before ready. Grouse should not be over-cooked but must be just cooked or on the verge of just being cooked through. Remove to a serving dish, still on the toast, and garnish with watercress and matchstick potatoes.

Use the pan juices, after removing the excess fat, to make a thin gravy to which 4-6 tablespoons red wine or port may be added. Also serve with fried breadcrumbs and/or bread sauce; a celery and apple salad along with a green vegetable make good accompaniments.
SERVES 2-3

Note: large birds will serve two; simply cut in half and remove the back bone.

GROUSE EN COCOTTE
Grouse braised on a bed of vegetables – ideal for mature birds.

> **2-4 mature grouse, oven ready**
> **Salt and pepper**
> **40g/1½oz butter or margarine**
> **2 onions, peeled and thinly sliced**
> **2 carrots, peeled and thinly sliced**
> **3-4 sticks celery, sliced**
> **1 turnip, peeled and diced**
> **1 bouquet garni**
> **300-400ml/½-¾ pint good stock**
> **½ level teaspoon dried thyme**
> **150ml/¼ pint red wine**
> **2 level tablespoons redcurrant or cranberry jelly**
> *To garnish:*
> **Fried croutons**
> **Watercress**
> **Lemon wedges**

Season the grouse inside and out with salt and pepper. Melt the butter or margarine in a large saucepan or flameproof casserole and brown the grouse all over; then remove from the pan. Add the vegetables to the pan, cover and cook over a very low heat, shaking frequently until beginning to colour lightly. Replace the grouse on top of the vegetables and add the bouquet garni. Season the stock and add sufficient just to cover the vegetables and add the thyme and wine. Bring slowly to the boil, cover tightly and simmer gently for 40 minutes, basting once or twice.

Remove the pan from the heat and place in a moderate oven (180°C/350°F, Gas Mark 4) for a further 30-40 minutes until very tender. Remove the grouse, split in half and cut away the backbone and place on a serving dish. Strain off the liquor, add redcurrant

BASIC ROAST GROUSE

GROUSE EN COCOTTE

jelly and boil to a syrupy consistency. Adjust seasonings and spoon over the grouse. Garnish with fried croutons, watercress and lemon wedges.
SERVES 4

POT ROAST OF GROUSE
(*pictured on page 41*)

4 young or old grouse, oven ready
Salt and pepper
175g/6oz bacon derinded and diced
2 tablespoons oil
12 button onions, peeled
6 carrots, peeled and thickly sliced
2 level teaspoons capers or
chopped stuffed olives
150 ml / ¼ pint stock
150 ml / ¼ pint cider
2 level teaspoons cornflour
To garnish:
Parsley

Wipe the grouse and season well. Fry the bacon in the oil until golden brown and remove to a large casserole. Brown the grouse in the same fat and add to the casserole. Fry the onions and carrots gently until lightly coloured and then spoon around the birds, together with the capers, seasonings, stock and cider.

Cover tightly with a lid or foil and cook in a moderate oven (180°C / 350°F, Gas Mark 4) for 1¼ – 1½ hours or until tender. Strain off the liquid, make up to 300ml / ½ pint if necessary with stock or cider and thicken with cornflour blended in a little cold water. Boil for 1-2 minutes, adjust seasonings and place in a sauceboat. Remove the birds to a serving dish, surround with vegetables and garnish with parsley.
SERVES 4

GROUSE WITH BLUEBERRIES
(*pictured on page 42*)

4 young grouse, oven ready
1 lemon, quartered
Salt and pepper
75g/3oz butter or margarine
2 tablespoons oil
Approx 2 tablespoons flour
175g/6oz blueberries
Grated rind of ½ lemon
1 tablespoon lemon juice
150ml/¼ pint water
4 rounds of toast
1 tablespoon clear honey
150ml/¼ pint stock

Wipe the grouse inside and out and put a piece of lemon in each cavity. Season lightly and stand in a roasting tin. Rub liberally with butter and then pour the oil overall. Cook for 30-45 minutes, depending on size, (220°C / 425°F, Gas Mark 7) basting often. Dredge the breasts lightly with a little flour after basting, about 10 minutes before ready.

Meanwhile put the blueberries into a small pan with the lemon rind, juice and water. Bring slowly to the boil and simmer for 2-3 minutes. Remove the grouse from the roasting tin and keep warm; then skim off any excess fat from the pan juices. Add the honey, stock and juices strained from the blueberries to the pan with the juices from cooking the grouse and bring up to the boil, stirring all the time. Simmer for 2 minutes, season to taste and strain. Add the blueberries and spoon a little over each grouse.

The cooked birds may be halved with the backbones removed and laid on a dish before pouring on the sauce.
SERVES 4

POT ROAST OF GROUSE

GROUSE WITH BLUEBERRIES

Grouse recipes

SPATCHCOCK OF GROUSE WITH ALMONDS

Young grouse can be spatchcocked or split open and then grilled, brushed with oil or a marinade to keep moist.

4 plump young grouse, oven ready
1 clove garlic, crushed
Oil
3 tablespoons lemon juice
Salt and pepper
75g/3oz butter or margarine
50g/2oz flaked almonds
$1/2$ level teaspoon finely grated lemon rind
1 level tablespoon freshly chopped parsley
To garnish:
Parsley sprigs
Fried bread triangles

Cut the grouse open along the backbone and press it out so that it lays flat with the flesh upwards. Rub lightly with garlic then brush with a mixture of 1 tablespoon each of oil and lemon juice and season with salt and pepper. Leave to marinate for about 30 minutes. Place the grouse on a grill rack lined with foil and cook under a moderate heat until well browned; turn over and cook the underside, brushing from time to time with the oil and lemon juice. It should take about 15 minutes until just cooked through and tender.

Meanwhile melt the butter and fry the almonds until lightly browned. Quickly add the remaining lemon juice and remove from the heat, then season and add the lemon rind and chopped parsley. Put the grouse on a serving dish and spoon over the sauce. Garnish with parsley and fried bread.
SERVES 4

ROAST GROUSE WITH JUNIPER SAUCE

For a change try serving this juniper sauce with roast young grouse. If the birds are mature they may be casseroled in it adding an extra 150ml/$1/4$ pint stock and allowing 1-1$1/2$ hours.

2-4 grouse, oven ready
Salt and pepper
Few streaky bacon rashers, derinded
Little oil, butter or margarine
1 small onion, peeled and quartered
Sauce:
50g/2oz streaky bacon, rashers, derinded and chopped
1 onion, peeled and finely chopped
2 sticks celery, finely chopped
1 tablespoon oil
1 level tablespoon dried juniper berries
300ml/$1/2$ pint stock
25g/1oz butter or margarine
25g/1oz flour
150ml/$1/4$ pint dry white wine
1 level tablespoon tomato purée
Lemon juice to taste

Begin the sauce first:
Sauté the bacon, onion and celery in the oil until beginning to colour.

Add the juniper berries and stock and bring to the boil. Cover and simmer gently for about 40 minutes.

Meanwhile prepare the grouse: season each with salt and pepper, cover each with fatty bacon and put a piece of onion in the cavities.

Place in a roasting tin with plenty of oil, butter or margarine and roast as usual in a hot oven (220°C/425°F, Gas Mark 7) for up to 40 minutes depending on size, basting frequently.

To complete the sauce, sieve or liquidise the vegetable mixture.

Melt the butter or margarine in a pan, stir in the flour and cook for a minute or so.

Gradually add the vegetable purée, wine and tomato purée and bring up to the boil, adding a little extra stock if too thick.

Season to taste and sharpen with lemon juice. Serve the grouse coated in the sauce and garnished with watercress and lemon.
SERVES 3-6

BREASTS OF GROUSE WITH WATER CHESTNUTS

Just the breasts are used for this recipe and they combine textures and flavour with water chestnuts and orange segments.

Use the carcase for soup.

4 grouse, oven ready
30g/1¹/2 oz butter
Salt and pepper
1 clove garlic, crushed
1 can water chestnuts, drained and sliced
Grated rind of 1 orange
Juice of 2 oranges
Segments of 2 oranges
150 ml/¹/4 pint dry white wine
To garnish:
Orange slices
Parsley

Remove the breasts carefully from the grouse using a sharp knife. Melt the fat in a pan and add the breasts and cook gently for 5-6 minutes each side until just cooked through.

Remove from the pan and keep warm. Add the garlic, water chestnuts,

and orange rind to the pan juices and stir well to heat through. Add the orange juice and segments and the wine and bring to the boil. Simmer gently for 3-4 minutes.

Season to taste and spoon over the grouse. Serve garnished with orange slices and parsley.
SERVES 4

BREASTS OF GROUSE WITH WATER CHESTNUTS
(pictured below)

Grouse recipes

GROUSE IN A POT

Pot roasting grouse in a wine sauce imparts a really good flavour to the birds.

4 grouse, oven ready
Salt and pepper
50g/2 oz butter or margarine
12-16 button onions, peeled
1 rasher bacon cut 1.5 cm/^{1}/$_2$ inch
thick, derinded and diced
300ml/^{1}/$_2$ pint red wine
2 tablespoons lemon juice
2 tablespoons redcurrant jelly
100-175g/4-6oz button mushrooms
4 rounds of toast
4 tablespoons double cream
To garnish:
Freshly chopped parsley or chives

Trim the grouse and season lightly. Melt the butter in a pan and brown the grouse all over. Transfer to a casserole just large enough to hold them. Fry the onions and bacon in the same fat until lightly browned and spoon around the grouse.

Add the wine, lemon juice and redcurrant jelly to the pan and bring to the boil. Boil until reduced by about a quarter, then season well and pour over the grouse. Cover and cook in a fairly hot oven (200ºC/400ºF, Gas Mark 6) for 30 minutes. Baste with the juices and add the mushrooms.

Cover again and return to the oven and stand on a serving dish. Keep warm. Spoon off any excess fat from the pan juices, add the cream and reheat gently. Adjust the seasonings and spoon a little sauce over each grouse and sprinkle with parsley and/or chives. Hand the rest of the sauce separately.
SERVES 4

GROUSE WITH GRAPE AND APPLE SAUCE

Fruit blends well with the richness of grouse. Here grapes and apples are combined.

4 grouse, oven ready
1 small lemon, quartered
salt and pepper
50g/2 oz softened butter or
margarine
4 rounds toast
2 tablespoons oil
Sauce:
1 level tablespoon flour
150ml/^{1}/$_4$ pint apple juice
150ml/^{1}/$_4$ pint stock
1 level teaspoon tomato purée
Juice of 1 lemon
1 tablespoon clear honey
1 dessert apple, cored and sliced
100g/4 oz small seedless green
grapes
To garnish:
Small bunches of grapes
Watercress

Wipe the grouse all over and put a quarter of lemon in the cavity of each bird. Season lightly and rub all over with softened fat. Stand each grouse on a round of toast and place in a roasting tin. Pour the oil over the birds and roast in a hot oven (220ºC/425ºF, Gas Mark 7) for 30-40 minutes, basting once or twice, until well browned and just cooked. Remove the birds on their croutes to a serving dish and keep warm. Spoon off any excess fat from the pan juices, then stir the flour into the residue. Cook for a minute or so then gradually add the apple juice, stock, tomato purée and lemon juice. Bring up to the boil and simmer for 2-3 minutes. Strain into a clean pan and

GROUSE IN A POT

GROUSE WITH GRAPE AND APPLE SAUCE

add the honey and seasonings to taste and the apple and grapes.

Reheat gently not letting the apple slices break up. Spoon a little over the grouse and serve the rest in a sauce boat. Garnish with bunches of grapes and watercress.
SERVES 4

GROUSE WITH GREEN OLIVES

Stuffed green olives give a Mediterranean flavour to grouse.

2 young grouse, oven ready
Salt and pepper
Streaky bacon
65g/ 2^{1}/$_{2}$ oz butter
1 onion, peeled and very finely chopped
3 lean back rashers bacon, derinded and cut into strips
75g/3oz stuffed green olives, halved
150ml/^{1}/$_{4}$ pint red wine
2 level teaspoons tomato purée
300ml/^{1}/$_{2}$ pint stock
2-3 teaspoons cornflour
Lemon juice
To garnish:
Fried bread triangles
Parsley sprigs

Season the grouse inside and out and cover the breasts with fat bacon, securing with fine string or cotton. Place in a roasting tin and cover with 40g /1^{1}/$_{2}$ oz butter. Roast in a hot oven (220°C/425°F, Gas Mark 7) for 30-40 minutes until cooked through, basting several times and removing fat bacon from the breasts for the last 10 minutes.

Meanwhile melt the remaining butter in a small pan and sauté the onion gently until soft but not coloured. Add the bacon and olives and continue for 2-3 minutes, then add the wine, tomato purée and stock and bring to the boil. Boil until reduced by one-third then thicken with the cornflour blended in a little cold water. Bring back to boil, adjust seasonings, sharpen with a little lemon juice and keep hot.

Split the grouse in half, removing the back bone, and place on a warm serving dish. Spoon the sauce over and garnish with fried bread and parsley.
SERVES 4

CRANBERRY GROUSE

A quick grilled recipe to use with young grouse (or partridges).

4 grouse, oven ready
Little oil
Salt and black pepper
Approx 6 level tablespoons bottled cranberry sauce
2 tablespoons red wine
Grated rind and juice of 1 orange
To garnish:
Orange slices

Split the grouse in half and brush liberally with oil. Season well and stand on a foil-lined grill rack. Cook under a preheated moderate grill for 5 minutes each side. Turn so the skin side is upwards.

Mix the cranberry sauce, wine, orange rind and juice and spoon over the grouse. Replace under the grill for about 5-10 minutes or until cooked through, spooning the cranberry mixture over the birds several times. Serve with the sauce spooned over and garnished with slices of orange.
SERVES 4

GROUSE WITH GREEN OLIVES

CRANBERRY GROUSE

Grouse recipes

BREAST OF GROUSE EN CROUTE

Instead of removing the flesh from the carcase when cooked, it can be done beforehand and the resulting bones used for soup or stock or the flesh removed to make a pâté.

4 grouse, oven ready
Salt and pepper
1 onion, peeled and chopped
3 tablespoons oil
Grated rind of $1/2$ orange
1 level tablespoon freshly chopped parsley
1 $1/2$ level teaspoons freshly chopped thyme

BREAST OF GROUSE EN CROUTE
(pictured below)

50g/2oz fresh breadcrumbs
8 rashers streaky bacon, derinded
350g/12oz puff pastry
Little beaten egg or top of the milk to glaze
To garnish:
Salads

Carefully remove the breasts from the grouse and, if liked, discard the skin. Season each lightly.

Fry the onion in 1 tablespoon oil until lightly browned then turn into a bowl and mix with the orange rind, parsley, thyme, seasonings and breadcrumbs. Spread a quarter of the stuffing over the inside of 4 pieces of grouse and sandwich together with the other pieces.

Stretch the bacon rashers with the back of a knife and wind around the parcels, attaching with wooden cocktail sticks or cotton, if necessary.

Heat the remaining oil and fry the parcels for about 5 minutes each side until browned and part cooked. Leave to cool and discard any cocktail sticks or cotton. Roll out the pastry thinly and cut into rectangles. Stand a grouse breast on each and wrap up to enclose completely, keeping the joins underneath and sticking together with water or beaten egg. Stand on a lightly greased baking sheet and glaze with beaten egg. Use the trimmings to make leaves and use to decorate the parcels; glaze again. Cook in a hot oven (220°C/425°F, Gas Mark 7) for 35-45 minutes, turning the oven down to moderately hot (190°C/375°F, Gas Mark 5) after about 25 minutes.

Serve hot or cold with cranberry sauce as an accompaniment. Garnish with salads.
SERVES 4

CAPERCAILLIE
COCK O' THE WOODS

THIS bird is by far the largest member of the grouse family and is also known as cock o' the woods or wood grouse.

It is also the largest of our gamebirds, though no game licence is needed to shoot it because it had become extinct in Britain when the game laws were framed in the 1830s. It was successfully reintroduced but is confined to Scotland where its diet includes a high proportion of coniferous tree shoots which give the flesh a rather unusual flavour. Some say it tastes of resin while others regard the meat highly.

Capercaillie is at its best in November and December before the birds have wasted due to severe weather and they should be hung for at least 2 weeks.

As large and sometimes long-lived birds, they are often tough so it is obviously better to cook only young birds and most people have a preference for the much smaller hens rather than the cocks.

In young birds the feet are supple and the legs soft and pliable while the feathers on the breast and under the wings are downy. This disappears with age and the legs become hard, rough and scaly – a definite sign of toughness!

For these birds it is advisable to use only long, slow methods of cooking, such as casseroles, or else use the cooked meat for pies. Roasting is a little uncertain and should only be tried if you are absolutely certain that your bird is young.

If the bird seems a little high before cooking add an onion studded with cloves to the body cavity, or if using portions then soak them in milk for 2 hours before cooking. Do not use the gizzard when making giblet stock as it has a strong and unpleasant flavour.

The recipes given here can also be used for mature larger grouse, but the cooking time will need to be cut down by 1/2-1 hour.

These recipes are best cooked and eaten at once, rather than being stored in the freezer, although the raw bird may be frozen as with other game.

CAPERCAILLIE WITH HARICOT BEANS
(pictured below, recipe on page 52)

Capercaillie recipes

CAPERCAILLIE WITH HARICOT BEANS

The beans need long cooking, which helps gives them a gamey flavour.

225g/8oz haricot beans, soaked
overnight in cold water
4 rashers streaky bacon, derinded
and chopped
2 large onion, peeled and chopped
2 level teaspoons salt
1¹/2 level teaspoons dry mustard
Freshly ground black pepper
2 level tablespoons black treacle
2 tablespoons vinegar
6 whole cloves
2 level teaspoons tomato purée
1 capercaillie, oven ready
2 tablespoons oil
To garnish:
Chopped parsley

Drain the beans and put them into a saucepan with fresh water to cover, bring up to the boil and simmer for an hour. Drain, reserving the liquor and transfer the beans to a large casserole. Add the bacon, onions, salt, mustard, plenty of pepper, treacle, vinegar, cloves and tomato purée and mix well.

Brown the capercaillie all over in the heated oil and then place on top of the beans, pressing it firmly into them. Add sufficient of the bean cooking liquor to cover the beans and then cover the casserole tightly, first with foil and then the lid. Cook in a moderate oven (180°C/350°F, Gas Mark 4) for an hour. Stir the beans, add a little more boiling bean liquor if necessary so the beans are just covered and replace the lid. Return to a cool oven (150°C/300°F, Gas Mark 3) and continue for 3 hours. Remove the capercaillie to a dish. Mix the beans,

discarding the cloves, and turn into a warmed dish. Sprinkle with chopped parsley and serve with slices of the bird and green vegetables or a salad.
SERVES 6

RED HOT CAPERCAILLIE CASSEROLE

This spicy sauce blends well with the flavour of the bird.

1 capercaillie, oven ready
2-3 tablespoons oil
3 large onions, peeled and finely
chopped
200g/7oz can pineapple pieces in
natural juice
2 level teaspoons medium curry
powder
1 level tablespoon tomato purée
425g/15oz can peeled tomatoes
2 tablespoons wine vinegar
2 level tablespoons apricot jam
300ml/¹/2 pint stock
Salt and pepper
To garnish:
Freshly chopped parsley

Cut the capercaillie into at least 8 portions. Heat 2 tablespoons of oil in a pan and brown the pieces all over. Transfer to a casserole. Fry the onions in the same pan, adding extra oil if necessary until soft but not coloured.

Chop the pineapple pieces finely and add to the pan with the juice and all the other ingredients. Bring up to the boil, stirring frequently, then pour over the capercaillie and cover tightly.

Cook in a moderate oven (160°C/325°F, Gas Mark 3) for about 2-2¹/2 hours until the bird is tender. Adjust seasonings, sprinkle with parsley and serve with boiled rice or pasta.
SERVES 4-6

CAPERCAILLIE WITH HARICOT BEANS
(pictured on page 51)

RED HOT CAPERCAILLIE CASSEROLE

CAPERCAILLIE CASSEROLE

There should be plenty on one bird to serve four.

1 capercaillie, oven ready and
jointed
40g/1¹/₂oz butter or margarine
1 tablespoon oil
100g/4oz lean bacon pieces,
derinded and chopped
225g/8oz pickling onions, peeled
2 cloves garlic, crushed
40g/1¹/₂oz flour
600ml/1 pint good game stock
4 tablespoons Marsala or sherry
Salt and pepper
2-3 level tablespoons cranberry
sauce
1 level tablespoon tomato purée
2 level tablespoons capers or
chopped gherkins
To garnish:
Parsley

Fry the pieces of capercaillie in the melted butter and oil until well browned. Transfer to an ovenproof casserole. Fry the bacon, onions and garlic in the same fat until lightly browned, then stir in the flour and cook for a minute or so. Gradually add the stock, Marsala or sherry and seasonings and bring up to the boil.

Add the cranberry sauce, tomato purée and capers and simmer for a couple of minutes. Pour over the capercaillie, cover and cook in a moderate oven (160°C/325°F, Gas Mark 3) for 1¹/₂-2 hours or until tender.

Adjust the seasonings and serve garnished with parsley and with mashed potatoes or boiled rice and a green vegetable.
SERVES 4

CAPERCAILLIE WITH HORSERADISH

The piquant flavour of horseradish makes a delicious casserole.

1 capercaillie, oven ready
Salt and pepper
1 level teaspoon ground coriander
1 level teaspoon ground ginger
2 tablespoon oil
16 pickling onions, peeled or
3 onions, peeled and cut into
quarters
4 sticks celery, sliced
25g/1oz flour
600ml/1 pint stock
1 tablespoon Worcestershire sauce
3-4 level tablespoons creamed
horseradish
4-6 tablespoons double cream
To garnish:
Celery leaves

Cut the capercaillie into at least 8 portions, season well and rub with coriander and ground ginger. Heat the oil in a pan and fry the pieces until browned all over; transfer to a casserole. Add the onions to the pan and fry until lightly browned then add the celery.

Stir in the flour and any remaining spices and cook for a minute or so. Gradually add the stock and bring up to the boil. Add seasonings, Worcestershire sauce and the horseradish and pour over the capercaillie. Cover tightly and cook in a moderate oven (160°C/325°F, Gas Mark 3) for 2 hours.

Adjust the seasonings, stir in the cream and return to the oven for about 20 minutes or until tender. Serve garnished with celery leaves.
SERVES 4-6

WOODCOCK AND SNIPE
DIMINUTIVE DELICACIES

BOTH OF these gamebirds are at their best from October to December. Snipe and woodcock are generally hung until they are rather high but this is a matter of personal preference and is not essential. Also the traditional way to cook and serve the birds is undrawn with the beak twisted round and used as a skewer for trussing.

They are quite difficult to pluck as the skin is very tender and particular care must be taken with the head, and the eyes should be removed. The gizzard should also be taken out but the alimentary canal or trail is all in one and when heated turns to liquid and becomes part of the accompaniment to the bird. However, many people draw and prepare their snipe and woodcock just as any other gamebird, roast them and still enjoy the taste but without all the excitement of preparing the birds to serve on toast with the trial as the delicacy.

The woodcock is by far the larger of the two and is considered by many people to be the best flavoured of all gamebirds. Small woodcock may also be served as a starter or savoury for a special dinner. However, snipe, too, is highly regarded by most people who have tried them. Whereas one woodcock might be sufficient for one person, two snipe each are recommended for a main course.

Both these waders are very susceptible to prolonged cold weather and will lose weight quickly during a freeze-up, but responsible sportsmen will not shoot the weakened birds during such conditions. It should be noted that the smaller jack snipe is protected and only the common snipe may be shot in mainland UK.

WOODCOCK WITH NORMANDY SAUCE

These small birds are best roasted in the usual way, but the sauces can be widely varied. Try this one which is an adaptation of a sauce usually served with pheasant.

4 woodcock, prepared
Salt and pepper
50g/2oz butter or margarine
2 tablespoons oil
4 rounds of bread
1 onion, peeled and finely chopped
1 cooking apple, peeled, cored and sliced
2 tablespoons brandy or Calvados
150ml/¼ pint single cream
To garnish:
Parsley
Orange slices

Wipe the birds all over and season well. Melt the butter and oil in a pan and fry the croutons of bread quickly until lightly browned. Stand a woodcock on each crouton in a roasting tin and baste with melted butter. Roast in a fairly hot oven (200°C/400°F; Gas Mark 6) for 20-30 minutes or until cooked through, basting several times. Remove from the tin to a serving dish, still on the croutons, and keep warm.

Transfer 2 tablespoons of the pan juices to a small saucepan and fry the onion gently until soft. Add the apple and continue until pulpy, adding a little water if necessary. Mash well, and then add the brandy followed by the cream and bring slowly just up to the boil. Season to taste and serve with the woodcock, garnished with parsley and orange slices.
SERVES 4

WOODCOCK WITH NORMANDY SAUCE
(pictured opposite)

Woodcock and Snipe recipes

WOODCOCK FORESTIERE

Here the cooked birds are split open and served on toast with the trail.

4 woodcock, prepared
Salt and pepper
25g/1oz butter or margarine
Little oil
1 leek, trimmed and cut into
julienne strips
3 carrots, peeled and cut into
julienne strips
1 courgette, trimmed and cut into
julienne strips
4 rounds of toast
150ml/¼ pint good stock
4-6 tablespoons sherry
Squeeze of lemon juice
1 level teaspoon redcurrant jelly
To garnish:
Fresh herbs

Wipe the woodcock all over and then rub with softened butter. Stand in a roasting tin and pour over a little oil. Cook in a fairly hot oven (200°C/400°F, Gas Mark 6) for 20-30 minutes until just cooked. Meanwhile blanch the leek in boiling water for a few minutes; cook the carrots in boiling water for 5 minutes and the courgette for a few minutes. Drain them all and toss together. Keep warm.

When the birds are ready, split them in half and spread the trail over the 4 pieces of toast. Put the woodcock onto the toast and keep warm. Add stock, sherry, lemon juice and redcurrant jelly to the pan juices after spooning off any excess fat and boil hard until reduced by about half. Season to taste. Arrange the vegetables around the woodcock and spoon the sauce over the birds. Garnish with fresh herbs.
SERVES 4

SNIPE EN CROUTE

Snipe are best roasted with their intestines – just remove the gizzard.

4 snipe, oven ready
4 rashers bacon
Salt and pepper
50g/2oz butter
350g/12oz puff pastry
Beaten egg to glaze
Orange Madeira Sauce:
1 level teaspoon freshly grated
orange rind
4 tablespoons Madeira
Juice of 3 oranges
1 level tablespoon redcurrant jelly
4 tablespoons stock
To garnish:
Orange slices and watercress

Wrap the bacon around the snipe and secure with string; then season well. Melt the butter in a pan and fry the birds until well sealed and browned all over. Remove from the pan and cool. Roll out the pastry, cut into four even-sized pieces and use each piece to enclose a snipe, damping and pressing the edges together. Stand in a lightly greased roasting tin with the joins underneath. Decorate with pastry trimming, glaze well and make a hole in the top of each for steam to escape. Cook in a hot oven (220°C/425°F, Gas Mark 7) for 25-30 minutes or until the pastry is well puffed up and golden brown.

Put all the sauce ingredients into the pan juices from frying the snipe, bring up to the boil, and boil uncovered until the sauce will glaze the back of a spoon. Adjust the seasonings and serve with the snipe garnished with orange and watercress.
SERVES 4

WOODCOCK
FORESTIERE

SNIPE EN CROUTE

GOLDEN PLOVER
TASTY WADER

THIS bird is more often cooked undrawn with the head skinned, eyes removed and beak used as a skewer, although the beak is not as long as that of snipe and woodcock. Remove the gizzard but leave the liver and trail in place. Allow at least one bird per person. Plovers are usually roasted and served on a croute of toast or fried bread which they may also be cooked on. They need only about 20 minutes in a fairly hot oven (200°C/400°F, Gas Mark 6) but plenty of basting is necessary. Garnish with watercress and serve with a piquant sauce or jelly such as cranberry or redcurrant.

PLOVERS A LA MAISON

Served on croutes of toast spread with pâté and a sauce with olives.

4 golden plovers, oven ready
8 rashers streaky bacon
Butter
Salt and pepper
4 croutes of toast or fried bread
75g/3oz smooth liver pâté
8-10 stuffed olives, sliced
1 level tablespoon freshly chopped parsley
Juice of 1/2 lemon
To garnish
Lemon and parsley

Wipe the prepared birds and wrap the bacon over the breasts, securing with wooden cocktail sticks if necessary. Spread a layer of softened butter over each bird, season well and stand in a buttered ovenproof dish. Cook in a fairly hot oven (200°C/400°F, Gas Mark 6) for about 30 minutes, basting once or twice, or until cooked through and tender. Spread each piece of toast or fried bread with the pâté and stand a bird on each, discarding the cocktail sticks. Place on a serving dish and keep warm.

Spoon off excess fat from the pan juices and add the olives. Toss over a gentle heat for a few minutes then stir in the parsley, lemon juice and a tablespoon of water. Season to taste, reheat and spoon over the birds. Garnish with lemon wedges and parsley.
SERVES 4

PLOVERS WITH CALVADOS

It is best to spread the trail onto fried croutons in this recipe.

4 plovers, oven ready
4 thin rashers streaky bacon
Salt and pepper
50g/2oz butter
4 rounds fried bread
4 tablespoons Calvados
2 tablespoons stock
2-3 tablespoons cream
(single or double)
To garnish
Watercress

Place the bacon over the plovers and season lightly. Melt the butter in a casserole just large enough to hold the birds and stand them in it. Baste and cook in a fairly hot oven (200°C/400°F, Gas Mark 6) for 20-30 minutes, basting once or twice, or until just cooked. Remove the birds to a serving dish. Spread the trail over the croutons of bread and put the birds on top; keep warm. Add the calvados and stock to the pan juices, boil hard for a few minutes, then season well, add the cream and pour over the birds. Serve at once garnished with watercress.
SERVES 4

PLOVERS A LA MAISON

PLOVERS WITH CALVADOS

WILD DUCK
A WIDE VARIETY

WILD duck is a convenient name for a wide variety of duck species. Of all the ducks which can be shot, the mallard (which was known individually as 'the wild duck' in olden times) is the best known and largest. It is a surface feeder along with wigeon, teal, gadwall (similar to mallard but much rarer), pintail and shoveler (which is not so good to eat as the others). Then there are the diving ducks, and the ones which can be shot legally are the tufted (which is regarded as the best for eating), goldeneye and pochard.

Wild duck have rather dry flesh, being virtually fat free (and thus good for those weight watching). Mallard are best cooked within 48 hours of shooting, though some people like to hang them for 1-2 days. Pluck, draw and truss as for a domestic duck and roast with extra fat, unlike a domestic duck which has plenty of its own fat. A mallard should serve 2-3 people. Wigeon and teal are much smaller and teal are rather more popular eating among sportsmen.

Often they are hung for 1-3 days but may be eaten fresh. Prepare as for mallard but adjust the cooking times accordingly. The other types of duck are not so common but should be prepared and cooked in the same way. These smaller birds will serve only 1-2 portions.

Duck coming from coastal areas sometimes have a 'marshy' or 'fishy' flavour. If you wish to get rid of this it can help to poach the bird in salted water for 15-20 minutes, then remove, wash and dry thoroughly; roast as usual but for less time as they are already part-cooked.

Roast wild duck should be served only barely cooked. This does not mean so underdone as to be raw and inedible, just pink-tinged, but if you do overcook the bird the flesh will become dry and gradually lose all its flavour and texture. It is all matter of preference, but if the bird is known to be mature then it is best to pot roast or at least cook in a longer moist way to prevent it being tough and dry.

All wild duck are suitable to freeze but should they have a strong flavour this will intensify during freezing, so take care with your choice of birds. Store raw birds for up to a year, cooked wild duck dishes for up to 2 months.

BREAST OF WILD DUCK WITH ORANGE AND GINGER
(Pictured left, recipe on page 69

TEAL WITH SPICED CELERY SAUCE
(Pictured below, recipe on page 64)

Wild duck recipes

BASIC ROAST WILD DUCK

2 wild duck (any variety), oven ready
Butter
2 orange quarters
Salt and pepper
Little port or orange juice (optional)
To garnish:
Watercress
Orange wedges

Prepare the ducks and wipe inside and out. Truss lightly and place a knob of butter and a piece of orange in the cavity of each bird. Season lightly, rub all over liberally with softened butter and place in a roasting tin. Cook in a hot oven (220°C/425°F, Gas Mark 7) allowing 30-50 minutes for mallard; 30-40 minutes for wigeon, and 20-30 minutes for teal and other small birds. Baste regularly and on no account allow to overcook.

Halfway through cooking a little port or orange juice may be poured over the birds. Serve on a warmed dish, garnished with watercress and orange wedges and serve with an orange salad and thin gravy made from the pan juices with the excess fat spooned off; or a Bigarade sauce (see recipe on page 62).

Wild ducks may be cooked at a lower temperature (180-200°C/350-400°F, Gas Mark 4-6), especially if they are to be glazed with honey or something which is likely to 'catch' in a hotter oven.

Increase the cooking times as required, but again take care not to overcook. Wild duck should be only just cooked, and some people prefer them underdone.
SERVES 2-6 *(depending on size of birds)*

WIGEON WITH CURACAO

An orange sauce with a difference is used to pot-roast these delicious birds.

4 wigeon, oven ready
2¹/₂ level tablespoons flour
1 level teaspoon celery salt
Salt and pepper
2 onions, peeled and chopped
175g/6oz button mushrooms, sliced
150ml/¹/₄ pint game or other stock
1 tablespoon soy sauce
3 tablespoons orange curacao liqueur
¹/₂ level teaspoon dried basil
3 oranges

Wipe the ducks inside and out. Combine the flour, celery salt and a little black pepper in a polythene bag and toss the ducks in this.

Place the ducks in a large ovenproof casserole. Sprinkle with the chopped onion and any remaining flour mixture, then sprinkle with the mushrooms.

Mix the stock, soy sauce, curacao, a little salt and the basil and bring up to the boil. Pour over the wigeon and cover tightly. Cook in a moderate oven (160°C/325°F Gas Mark 3) for 1¹/₄ hours or until tender.

Meanwhile peel and slice the oranges and heat gently in the oven with a little caster sugar sprinkled over them, if liked.

To serve, place one wigeon on each plate and garnish with slices of orange and spoon some of the sauce overall. Serve the remaining sauce separately in a jug.
SERVES 4

BREASTS OF WILD DUCK EN CROUTE

This dish can be prepared in advance, and cooked when required.

2 mallard or 4 teal, oven ready
25g/1oz butter
1 onion, peeled and finely chopped
2 duck livers
175g/6oz lean back bacon, derinded and chopped
Finely grated rind of 1 orange
8-10 stuffed olives, chopped or 75g/3oz button mushrooms, chopped
1-2 tablespoons port or brandy
1 tablespoon freshly chopped parsley
Salt and pepper
450g/1lb puff pastry
Beaten egg or milk to glaze

Prepare and roast the birds as usual but only until just over half cooked – about 20 minutes. Cool a little then remove each breast carefully; cut each breast in half if using mallard. Melt the butter and fry the onion until soft. Add the chopped livers, bacon and orange rind and continue until soft.

Stir in the olives or mushrooms, port or brandy, seasonings and parsley and leave to cool. Roll out the pastry thinly on a floured surface and cut into eight squares large enough to enclose a duck breast. Put the breasts onto the pastry and spread a little bacon mixture on top of each one.

Damp the edges of the pastry and bring together in an envelope shape to enclose the filling. Press edges well together and put onto a dampened backing sheet with pastry seams underneath. Decorate with the pastry trimmings cut into leaves and glaze well. Cook in a hot oven (220°C/425°F Gas Mark 7) for 25-30 minutes or until the pastry is puffy and golden brown.

Serve with a gravy made with the pan juices, flavoured with the juice and grated rind of 1 orange, juice of 1/2 lemon, 3 tablespoons red wine, 2 tablespoons redcurrant or rowan jelly, seasonings and a little stock.
SERVES 8

HONEY GLAZED TEAL

Wild duck are supposed to be served pink-tinged, but many people do not care for this, so the cooking times are flexible to allow for all tastes.

4 teal, oven ready
6 sprigs fresh thyme
Approx 75g/3oz butter
Salt and pepper
4 tablespoons clear honey
To garnish:
Mixed lettuce leaves
Sprigs of fresh herbs
Lemon wedges

Put a sprig of thyme and small knob of the butter inside the cavity of each bird. Finely chop the remaining thyme. Season the birds with salt and pepper and stand in a roasting tin. Melt the remaining butter and honey together and pour over the birds and sprinkle with some of the chopped thyme. Roast in a fairly hot oven (200°C/400°F, Gas Mark 6) for 30-35 minutes, basting once or twice with the juices. Transfer each bird to a serving plate and garnish with mixed lettuces, fresh herbs and lemon wedges. Spoon excess fat from the pan juices, add the remaining chopped thyme and spoon over the birds. Serve with new potatoes.
SERVES 4

BREASTS OF WILD DUCK EN CROUTE

HONEY GLAZED TEAL

Wild duck recipes

WILD DUCK WITH BIGARADE SAUCE

This is a traditional orange sauce served with all types of wild duck. Seville oranges, when available, give the true flavour, but ordinary oranges and a splash of lemon juice make a very good substitute.

2 wild ducks, oven ready
A little softened butter
Salt and pepper
2 lemons
3 oranges
1 level tablespoon brown sugar
1 tablespoon wine vinegar
2 tablespoons brandy or port
1-2 level teaspoons cornflour
Little stock
To garnish:
Watercress and orange slices

Spread the ducks all over with softened butter and season well. Place a knob of butter and 2 quarters of lemon in each cavity and place in a roasting tin. Add a little more butter to the tin and cook in a hot oven (220°C/ 425°F, Gas Mark 7) allowing about 20-30 minutes for small ducks or 30-60 minutes for larger birds, basting frequently. Take care not to overcook or the flesh will become dry.

Meanwhile for the sauce, finely grate the rind from one orange and squeeze the juice from all the oranges and the remaining lemon.

Melt the sugar in a pan with the vinegar and heat gently until it turns to a darkish brown caramel – but do not let it burn. Add the fruit juices and brandy and simmer gently for about 2 minutes. Remove the ducks from the tin and keep warm. If liked they may be cut into portions.

Skim off the excess fat from the pan drippings, then add the grated orange rind and the orange sauce. Bring slowly to the boil, stirring continuously. Blend the cornflour with a little cold water, add to the sauce and bring back to the boil. Simmer gently for 2-3 minutes, adding a little extra stock, if necessary.

Season to taste and serve in a sauce boat with the ducks garnished with watercress and orange, or, if cut into portions, spoon the sauce over the pieces of duck and garnish.
SERVES 4

WILD DUCK WITH BIGARADE SAUCE
(pictured below)

WILD DUCK WITH PORT AND CRANBERRY SAUCE

If fresh cranberries are unavailable, use frozen ones or substitute with half a small jar of cranberry sauce (not jelly) and 1 tablespoon lemon juice.

2 mallard or wigeon or 4 teal, oven ready
Salt and pepper
1 orange, quartered
40g/1¹/2oz butter or margarine
3 tablespoons oil
1 level tablespoon flour
150ml/¹/4 pint port
150ml/¹/4 pint good stock
100g/4oz cranberries fresh or frozen
Grated rind and juice of 1 orange
1 level tablespoon molasses or dark muscovado sugar

Wipe the ducks inside and out, season lightly and put the pieces of orange inside the cavity. Stand in a roasting tin and rub all over with butter or margarine and then pour the oil overall. Cook in a hot oven (220°C/425°F, Gas Mark 7) allowing 30-60 minutes, depending on size, and basting at least twice. Transfer to a serving dish and keep warm.

Spoon off excess fat from the pan juices, leaving about a tablespoonful. Stir the flour into the juices and cook for a minute or so. Gradually add the port and stock and bring to the boil. Add the cranberries, orange rind and juice and the sugar and simmer gently until the fruit is very tender – about 5 minutes. Adjust the seasonings and serve with a little of the sauce spooned over the birds and the rest separately in a jug. Serve garnished with parsley or watercress.
SERVES 4

WILD DUCK WITH GRAPEFRUIT

Roasted halved ducks, quicker to cook than whole birds, given a tangy flavour with grapefruit sections and marmalade

2 small wild ducks, oven ready
Butter
1 onion, peeled and finely chopped
Salt and pepper
1 large or 2 small grapefruit
2 level tablespoons chunky marmalade
4 tablespoons stock
To garnish:
Watercress
Black olives

Cut the ducks in half and rub each piece with butter. Stand in a roasting tin and sprinkle with the onion. Season lightly. Roast in fairly hot oven (200°/400°F, Gas mark 6) for 25 minutes, basting occasionally, or until tender.

Meanwhile pare the rind from half a grapefruit with a potato peeler and cut into narrow strips. Cook in boiling water for 5 minutes and drain. Cut away the pith from the grapefruit and carefully ease out the segments from between the membranes.

When ready remove the duck to a serving dish and keep warm. Spoon off excess fat from the pan juices and add the grapefruit segments, strips of rind and the marmalade dissolved in the stock. Bring slowly to the boil and simmer for 4-5 minutes taking care the grapefruit does not break up. Adjust seasonings and spoon over and around the duck. Garnish with watercress and black olives.
SERVES 4

WILD DUCK WITH PORT AND CRANBERRY SAUCE

WILD DUCK WITH GRAPEFRUIT

Wild duck recipes

LEMON GLAZED WILD DUCK

A lemon glaze containing julienne strips of peel spooned over roasted duck with a herb and spice stuffing.

1 mallard or 2 smaller wild duck, oven ready
50g/2oz fresh white breadcrumbs
1 level tablespoon grated onion
2 level tablespoons fresh chopped parsley
1 level tablespoon dried thyme
Pinch each of garlic powder and ground nutmeg
Salt and pepper
Finely grated rind of 1/2 lemon
1 small dessert apple, peeled, cored and coarsely grated
1 tablespoon lemon juice
1 egg yolk
25g/1oz butter or margarine
Glaze:
150ml/1/4 pint medium cider
150ml/1/4 pint stock
1 lemon
1/2 level teaspoon cornflour
2-3 teaspoons lemon juice
To garnish:
Watercress

Wipe the duck inside and out. Combine the breadcrumbs, onion, parsley, thyme, garlic, nutmeg, seasonings, lemon rind and grated apple and bind together with the lemon juice and egg yolk. Use to stuff the neck end of the bird and put the excess into the cavity.

Rub the bird all over with softened butter and season with salt and pepper. Stand in a greased roasting tin or dish and cook in fairly hot oven (200°C/400°F, Gas Mark 6) for about an hour (depending on size) or until just tender and basting once or twice during cooking. Remove the duck to a serving dish and keep warm.

Spoon the excess fat from the pan juices and add the cider and stock to the residue. Pare the rind off the lemon using a potato peeler and cut into julienne strips. Simmer gently in the cider mixture for above 5 minutes until tender.

Meanwhile cut off the excess pith from the lemon and cut the lemon into thin slices, discarding any pips. Arrange these in a line down the centre of the duck.

Thicken the pan juices with the cornflour blended in the lemon juice and return to the boil for a minute or so. Adjust seasonings, add a pinch of sugar if liked, and spoon the sauce over the duck (including the strips of peel). Garnish with watercress.
SERVES 3-4

TEAL WITH SPICED CELERY SAUCE (*pictured on page 59*)
Coriander and cumin blend well with the special flavour of wild duck.

4 teal, oven ready
1 orange, quartered
50g/2oz butter or margarine
2 tablespoons oil
Salt and pepper
1/2 head celery, finely sliced
1-2 cloves garlic, crushed
1 small onion, peeled and finely chopped
1/2 level teaspoon ground coriander
1/4 level teaspoon ground cumin
150ml/1/4 pint stock
150ml/1/4 pint cream, single or double
To garnish:
Celery leaves

LEMON GLAZED WILD DUCK

TEAL WITH SPICED CELERY SAUCE

Put a quarter of orange in the cavity of each bird, wipe all over and stand in a small roasting tin. Rub with butter, pour the oil overall and season lightly. Roast in a hot oven (220°C/425°F, Gas Mark 7) for 25-30 minutes, basting at least once, until just cooked through. If you prefer your duck well done, continue for an extra 5-10 minutes, but take care not to overcook. Remove the birds and keep warm.

Spoon off 2-3 tablespoons fat from the cooking juices to a saucepan and fry the celery, garlic and onion gently until soft. Discard the rest of the fat from the pan juices and add the celery mixture to these juices. Mix in the coriander, cumin and seasonings and cook gently for a minute or so, then gradually add the stock and bring to the boil.

Cook until most of the liquid has been evaporated then add the cream and reheat gently. Adjust the seasonings and serve each bird on a bed of the celery sauce with a garnish of celery leaves.
SERVES 4

Note: the spices may be increased for a stronger flavour, if preferred.

JOANNE'S DUCK

Portions of wild duck cooked with cider and brandy and topped with a crispy fried breadcrumb and hazelnut mixture.

2 mallard or 3 smaller wild duck, oven ready
Little seasoned flour
Butter and/or oil for frying
1 onion, peeled and finely chopped
1 clove garlic, crushed
1 carrot, peeled and coarsely grated
300ml/1/2 pint dry cider
2 tablespoons brandy
4 level tablespoons fresh breadcrumbs
50g/2oz hazelnuts or walnuts, chopped
To garnish:
Fried mushrooms
Parsley sprigs
Cherry tomatoes

Halve or quarter each duck and coat in seasoned flour. Melt a little butter and/or oil in a pan and fry the pieces of duck gently until well browned all over and almost cooked through.

Meanwhile melt 40g/1 1/2oz butter in another pan and fry the onions and garlic gently until soft, Add the carrots and continue for a minute or so, then stir in 1 level tablespoon of the seasoned flour and mix well.

Add the cider and bring up to the boil. Place the duck in the pan, warm the brandy and pour over the ducks, then ignite. Cover pan and simmer gently for about 15 minutes, stirring occasionally until tender. A little extra stock or water may be needed; then adjust the seasonings. Keep warm while preparing the garnish.

Melt about 40g/1 1/2oz butter in a pan and fry the breadcrumbs gently until a pale golden brown, stirring almost continuously.

Add the nuts and continue for a few minutes longer. Arrange the duck portions on a serving dish with the sauce spooned over and around and sprinkle the crispy breadcrumb nut mixture overall.

Garnish with mushrooms, parsley and cherry tomatoes.
SERVES 6

JOANNE'S DUCK

Wild duck recipes

WILD DUCKS WITH GINGER

Roasted spicy wild ducks, served with glazed apple rings and a ginger, redcurrant and port sauce.

2 mallard or 4 smaller duck, oven ready
50-75g/2-3oz butter or margarine
Salt and pepper
1/2 level teaspoon ground ginger
1 bouquet garni
1 clove garlic, crushed
4 dessert apples
4 tablespoons redcurrant jelly
2 tablespoons wine vinegar
3-4 pieces stem ginger, finely chopped
Juice of 1 large orange
100ml/4fl oz port
To garnish:
Watercress or parsley

Brown the prepared ducks in the melted butter in a large pan. Transfer to a roasting tin and season the skins with salt, pepper and ginger and pour half the fat from frying the ducks over them. Add the bouquet garni and garlic and cover with foil. Cook in a hot oven (200°/400°CF, Gas Mark 6) for about 30 minutes. Peel the apples, remove cores with a corer and then cut in half. Brown the apples in the remaining fat in the pan then place around the ducks.

Return to the oven for about 10 minutes, uncovered or until tender and browned. Dissolve the redcurrant jelly in the vinegar and keep warm. Remove ducks to a serving dish and surround with the apples.

Glaze both the ducks and apples with the redcurrant mixture and keep warm. Skim the fat from the pan juices and add the chopped ginger, orange juice, port and any remaining redcurrant glaze. Bring to the boil, simmer briefly, adjust seasonings and serve in a sauce boat. Garnish with watercress or parsley.
SERVES 4-6

WIGEON WITH DATE AND ORANGE STUFFING

Sometimes a stuffing is just what is required to make a good dish even better. With these birds it is possible to cut them in half when cooked giving half the stuffing to each portion.

2 wigeon or 4 teal, oven ready
Salt and pepper
Stuffing:
1 small onion, peeled and finely chopped
25g/1oz butter or margarine
75g/3oz stoned dates, finely Chopped grated rind of 1 orange
50g/2oz fresh breadcrumbs
1 level teaspoon dried thyme
1 level tablespoon freshly chopped parsley
Good pinch of ground allspice
Beaten egg and/or orange juice to bind
4 tablespoons oil
To garnish:
Fresh herbs
Orange wedges

Wipe the ducks inside and out and season lightly. For the stuffing, fry the onion gently in the melted fat till soft. Add the dates and 2-3 tablespoons water and cook until soft and the liquid is absorbed. Turn into a bowl, add the orange rind and leave to cool. Mix in the breadcrumbs, thyme, parsley, seasonings and allspice and add sufficient egg and/or orange juice to bind. Divide between the birds putting stuffing into the cavity. Stand in a roasting tin and pour the oil overall. Season lightly, if liked, and then cook in a hot oven (220°C/425°F, Gas Mark 7) for 30-40 minutes, basting several times during cooking, until tender. Take care not to overcook.

Transfer to a serving dish and garnish with fresh herbs and orange wedges. Skim off the excess fat from the pan juices and add stock and seasonings to make a thin gravy.
SERVES 4

MALLARD WITH AVOCADO DRESSING

An unusual way to serve cold wild duck, which can be used for a specially cooked duck or the leftovers.

2 mallard, roasted and cooled
$1/2$ level teaspoon grated lemon rind
3 spring onions, trimmed and sliced
1 small clove garlic, crushed
2 ripe avocados
2 tablespoons lemon juice
150ml/$1/4$pt soured cream
3 tablespoons thick mayonnaise
Salt and pepper
1 level tablespoon freshly chopped parsley
1 level teaspoon freshly chopped tarragon or pinch of dried tarragon
To garnish:
Lettuce leaves and cherry tomatoes

Carve the flesh from the ducks, keeping the wings and legs intact, if preferred. Arrange in an even layer on a serving dish. Put the lemon rind, onions and garlic into a food processor or blender and switch on until well

chopped. Add one peeled and sliced avocado and 1 tablespoon lemon juice and switch on until smooth. Add soured cream and mayonnaise and process again. Season to taste. Stir in the herbs and then spoon the sauce evenly over the duck.

Cover and chill for 2 hours. Serve garnished with lettuce leaves, slices of the remaining avocado dipped in lemon juice, and cherry tomatoes.
SERVES 4-5

**MALLARD WITH
AVOCADO DRESSING**
(pictured below)

Wild duck recipes

WILD DUCK FLAN
These can also be made into small flans by lining four individual Yorkshire pudding tins or 10cm/4in flan tins.

1 wild duck, roasted (or other game birds)
150g/6oz shortcrust pastry (made using 150g/6oz plain flour etc)
150ml/¹/₄ pint mayonnaise or a mixture of mayonnaise and fromage frais or soured cream
150ml/¹/₄ pint liquid aspic jelly
2 level tablespoons freshly chopped parsley
2 level tablespoons snipped chives or spring onions
Salt and pepper
Squeeze of lemon or lime juice
To garnish:
Sliced cucumber
Stuffed olives
Lemon or lime wedges

Roll out the pastry and use to line a 20cm/8in flan tin or ring. Decorate or trim the edges, prick the base and bake blind in a fairly hot oven (200°C/400°F, Gas Mark 6) for 20 minutes; remove the paper and baking beans and return to the oven for about 5 minutes to dry out. Cool.

For the filling, combine the mayonnaise or mixture with aspic jelly, parsley, chives or spring onions, seasonings and a squeeze or lemon or lime juice. Leave until beginning to thicken but not set. Remove the flesh from the duck and cut into narrow strips; then arrange evenly in the pastry case. Spoon the sauce evenly over the game and chill until set. Before serving, remove the flan from the tin if possible, and stand on a serving plate. Garnish with slices of cucumber, stuffed olives and lemon or lime wedges.
SERVES 4-6

MALLARD WITH CARIBBEAN LIME SAUCE
A tangy lime and lemon sauce flavoured with honey and rum to serve with large or small wild duck.

2 mallard or other wild duck
2 lemons
2 limes
50g/2oz butter or margarine
1-2 tablespoons oil
Salt and pepper
300ml/¹/₂ pint stock
1-2 tablespoons honey
1-2 tablespoons dark rum
To garnish:
Slices of lemon and lime
Watercress

Quarter one of the lemons and place two pieces in the cavity of each bird. Stand in a roasting tin and spread all over with softened butter and then pour the oil overall: season if liked. Cook in a hot oven (220°C/425°F, Gas Mark 7) allowing 30-50 minutes, depending on the size and basting at least twice, until just cooked through, but in no way overcooked.

Pare the rind thinly from the limes using a potato peeler; cut into narrow strips and cook in boiling water for 5 minutes. Grate the rind from the remaining lemon and squeeze the juice from limes and lemon. When the birds are cooked, remove to a serving dish and keep warm. Spoon off any excess fat from the pan juices then add the rinds, juices and stock and bring up to the boil. Boil until reduced by almost

WILD DUCK FLAN

MALLARD WITH CARIBBEAN LIME SAUCE

half and the sauce is slightly syrupy. Stir in the honey, rum if used, seasonings and strips of lime rind and heat until the honey melts. Spoon over or serve with the ducks and garnish with slices of lemon, lime and watercress.
SERVES 4

WILD DUCK WITH CAPERS

Pot roast small, wild ducks cut in half to give two portions with a rich tomato and caper sauce – ideal for more mature birds.

2 teal or wigeon, oven ready
25g/1oz butter
Salt and pepper
1 large onion,
peeled and thinly sliced
425g/15oz can tomatoes
1 level tablespoon capers
1 tablespoon lemon juice
250ml/scant 1/4 pint white wine,
cider or stock
1/2 level teaspoon brown sugar
To garnish:
game chips and watercress

Brown the ducks in the melted butter quickly, then remove from the pan and season lightly . Fry the onion in the same pan until lightly browned. Pour off any excess fat and add the tomatoes, capers, lemon juice, wine and sugar and bring up to the boil. Place the ducks in a casserole, season the sauce and pour over. Cover tightly and cook in a fairly hot oven (200ºC/400ºF, Gas Mark 6) for about 25 minutes. Remove lid, baste the birds with a little of the juices in the casserole and continue, uncovered, for about 10 minutes or until tender. If liked the sauce may be puréed in a food processor or liquidiser to serve with the ducks which should be place on a serving dish and garnished with game chips and watercress.
SERVES 4

BREAST OF WILD DUCK WITH ORANGE AND GINGER
(pictured on page 58)

Choose one of the larger varieties of duck for this dish if possible.

4-6 mallard breasts, with skin on
50g/2oz butter
1 tablespoon oil (preferably walnut)
1 clove garlic, crushed
1 1/2 level teaspoons finely grated root ginger
4 spring onions, trimmed and sliced
Grated rind of 1 orange
150ml/1/4 pint fresh orange juice
150ml/1/4 pint dry white wine
Salt and pepper
To garnish:
Orange slices and watercress

Carefully remove the breasts from the ducks keeping the skin on if possible. Melt the butter and oil in a large pan and fry the breasts gently until partly cooked. Remove from the pan. Add the garlic, ginger and onions to the pan and cook gently for 2-3 minutes. Add the orange rind and juice and wine and bring to the boil. Season and replace the duck. Cover and simmer for about 15 minutes.

Remove the breasts, slice each into 3 or 4 pieces and arrange on a plate. Boil the juices to reduce a little and then spoon over the slices of duck. Garnish with orange slices and watercress.
SERVES 4-6

WILD DUCK
WITH CAPERS

BREAST OF WILD
DUCK WITH ORANGE
AND GINGER

WILD GOOSE
FOUR SPECIES

THERE are four species of wild goose which can be shot in Britain. Of these the largest is the Canada goose and this variety is about twice the size of the 'grey' geese. The three grey geese are the greylag, pinkfooted and whitefronted.

The Canada goose is probably the most popular of them all to eat with the tastiest and most tender flesh, but they are all excellent with individual flavours which 'grow' on one. With all geese the flesh is very dry as the birds lack fat so it needs plenty of extra fat added during cookery, both in the form of basting and as fat laid over the breast. Some people prefer to add about 300 ml/^{1}/$_2$ pint stock, wine or cider to the roasting tin to add moisture during cooking, and it is advisable to add a quartered orange or apple to the body cavity, again to add moisture.

Geese can be hung for about a week, though some people prefer to leave them for up to three weeks – it is a matter of personal taste. But do pay special attention to the weather and the conditions under which the geese have been transported and stored. For example, most wild geese will have been shot in northern Britain and after a day or two of travelling back by car (probably heated during the shooting season) no hanging at all is recommended for the average palate.

Do not bother to cook very old geese; the flesh can be tainted and will definitely be tough, but young birds which are recognisable by a pliable underbill and more brightly coloured legs make good eating and can be roasted or casseroled.

The recipes can be used for all sizes of goose, but adapt the cooking times accordingly. An average Canada goose will serve 6-8 portions but the grey geese are usually sufficient for only about 4 portions. Wild geese are suitable to freeze, but they are not very easy to obtain unless you have access to or know where to shoot them. It is illegal to sell all wild geese.

CIDERED GOOSE

A pot roast for goose with water chestnuts to give a 'bite' to the sauce.

1 young wild goose, oven ready
1 orange, quartered
1 lemon, quartered
1 small onion, peeled and quartered
Slices of pork fat or fatty bacon
300ml/^{1}/$_2$ pint stock (made from the giblets)
450ml/^{3}/$_4$ pint dry cider
Salt and pepper
2-3 sprigs fresh thyme
25g/1oz butter or margarine, melted
175g/6oz button mushrooms
125g/5oz can water chestnuts, sliced
40g/1^1/$_2$oz butter or margarine
40g/1^1/$_2$oz flour
To garnish:
Fresh thyme and parsley

Prepare the goose as for roasting and put the orange, lemon and onion in the cavity. Tie the pork fat or bacon over the breast and place in a roasting tin, breast downwards. Heat the stock and cider to just below boiling, season and pour over the goose. Add the thyme and cover with foil. Cook in a fairly hot oven (200°C/400°F, Gas Mark 6) for 30 minutes.

Reduce the temperature to moderate (180°C/350°F, Gas Mark 4), baste the bird well and continue cooking,

CIDERED GOOSE

covered, for about 1 hour, basting several times. Remove foil and pork fat and turn the goose breast upwards. Brush with melted fat and season with salt and pepper.

Add the mushrooms and water chestnuts to the roasting tin and cook for a 30-40 minutes, uncovered, until tender. Increase the oven temperature again for the last 10-15 minutes to crisp up the skin.

Place goose on a serving dish, drain mushrooms and water chestnuts and place around the bird. Skim any fat from the pan juices then boil until reduced to 450ml/³/₄ pint; keep warm. Melt the fat in a pan, stir in the flour and cook for a minute.

Gradually add the stock and bring up to the boil for 2 minutes. Adjust the seasonings and strain into a sauce boat. Garnish the goose with fresh herbs.
SERVES 6-8

Note: large wild ducks are good served this way too, but cut the middle cooking time to about 30 minutes.

WILD GOOSE A LA GRECQUE

Wild goose is best roasted with stock added to the roasting tin to keep the flesh moist, and this is a good idea when cooking domestic goose too.

1 wild goose, oven ready and trussed (with the giblets)
Little oil
Salt and pepper
1 onion, peeled and thinly sliced
1 bouquet garni
150ml/¹/₄ pint red wine
1 level tablespoon tomato purée
4-6 tablespoons double cream (optional)

Dolmas:
25g/1oz butter or margarine
1 clove garlic, crushed
1 small onion, peeled and chopped
3 tablespoons cooked rice
2 tomatoes, peeled and chopped
50g/2oz mushrooms, chopped
¹/₂ level teaspoon dried basil
12 vine leaves or small cabbage leaves, blanched

Use all the giblets except the liver to make about 300ml/¹/₂ pint stock. Prepare the goose and stand in a roasting tin. Brush lightly all over with the oil and season well. Pour the stock around the bird, adding the onions and bouquet garni. Cook in a moderate oven (180°C/350°F, Gas Mark 4) for about ³/₄-1¹/₄ hours, basting occasionally.

Meanwhile make the dolmas: chop the raw liver, cooked gizzard and heart, and fry in the melted butter with the garlic and onion until soft. Mix into the rice with the tomatoes, mushrooms, basil and seasonings.

Divide the rice mixture between the vine or cabbage leaves and roll up to enclose the filling. Secure with wooden cocktail sticks if necessary, then arrange around the goose in the stock. Continue to roast for 15-20 minutes until tender, basting once or twice.

When cooked, remove the goose and dolmas to a serving dish and keep warm. Strain the pan juices into a saucepan and add the wine and tomato purée and a little more stock or water if necessary; then simmer gently for 5 minutes. Adjust the seasonings, stir in the cream if used, reheat and serve in a sauce boat with the goose.
SERVES 6-8 *(depending on size)*

Wild Goose recipes

GOOSE WITH RED PLUMS

Again the goose is cooked breast downwards, the juices of the plums together with spices are used to flavour this recipe.

1 young wild goose, oven ready
1 orange, quartered
1 lemon, quartered
300ml/^{1}/$_2$ pint stock (made from the giblets)
550g/1^1/$_4$lb can red plums
1 onion, peeled and thinly sliced
2 teaspoons Worcestershire sauce
1-2 cloves garlic, crushed
2 tablespoons wine vinegar
Salt and pepper
1 level tsp ground cinnamon
Cornflour
To garnish:
Watercress and orange slices

Prepare the goose as for roasting and put the orange and lemon in the cavity. Place in a roasting tin, breast downwards.

Heat the stock and the juice from the can of plums to boiling, then add the onion, Worcestershire sauce, garlic, vinegar and plenty of seasonings and pour over the goose. Cover with foil and cook in a fairly hot oven (200°C/400°F, Gas Mark 6) for 30 minutes. Reduce the temperature to moderate (180°C/350°F, Gas Mark 4), baste the bird well and continue cooking, covered, for about 1 hour, again basting several times.

Remove foil and turn the goose breast upwards. Add the plums to the roasting tin with the cinnamon and cook uncovered for about 30 minutes, increasing the temperature again for the last 15 minutes to brown up the skin.

Remove the goose to a serving dish and thicken the juices, with the plums and onions still in it, with 2-3 level teaspoons cornflour blended in a little cold water.

Adjust the seasonings and serve with the goose, garnished with watercress and orange slices.
SERVES 6-8

ROAST GOOSE WITH RED CABBAGE

A prune and apple stuffing will help keep the flesh of the bird moist as well as give flavour. Red cabbage is a good accompaniment to all types of game.

1 wild goose, oven ready and trussed (with giblets)
225g/8oz no-need-to-soak prunes, stoned
450g/1lb cooking apples
1 small onion, peeled and finely chopped
Salt and pepper
Juice of 1 lemon
1-2 tablespoons oil
2 level tablespoons redcurrant or cranberry jelly
4-6 tablespoons red wine
2 level teaspoons cornflour
To garnish:
Lemon slices and watercress
Red Cabbage:
25g/1oz butter or margarine
1 small onion, peeled and finely chopped
900g/2lb red cabbage
25g/1oz brown sugar
75ml/3fl oz white or red wine vinegar
75ml/3fl oz water
Salt and pepper
1 cooking apple, peeled, cored and chopped

Use all the giblets except the liver to make about 450ml/$^3/_4$ pint stock. If necessary soak the prunes overnight in water, then drain, halve and remove the stones; then roughly chop the flesh. Peel, core and coarsely chop the apples and mix with the prunes together with the onion and seasonings. Wipe the bird inside and out and spoon the stuffing into the cavity. Stand the goose in a roasting tin, rub all over with half the lemon juice, then brush with oil and season well. Pour about 300ml/$^1/_2$ pint stock around the goose and cook in a moderate oven (180°C/350°F, Gas Mark 4) for about 1$^1/_2$ hours, basting occasionally, until cooked through and tender – the exact time depends on the size of the bird. When ready, remove to a serving dish and keep warm.

Spoon off excess fat from the pan juices, add remaining lemon juice, redcurrant jelly, a little more stock if necessary, and the wine and bring up to the boil, stirring until the jelly dissolves. Thicken with the cornflour blended in a little cold water and bring back to the boil for 2-3 minutes, adjust the seasonings. Serve goose garnished with lemon and watercress and with the sauce separately.

Meanwhile to prepare the cabbage, melt the butter in a saucepan and fry the onion gently until soft. Shred the cabbage, discarding any outer leaves and tough stalks, and add to the pan with the sugar, vinegar and water and mix thoroughly. Bring to the boil, cover and simmer very gently for about 40 minutes, stirring from time to time and adding extra boiling water if necessary to keep the cabbage moist. Season and serve with the goose.
SERVES 6 plus

WILD GOOSE PÂTÉ

The flavour of this pâté is at its best if the goose liver is added.

$^1/_2$ wild goose, skinned and boned
75g/3oz pork fat
175g/6oz bacon, derinded
Goose liver
2 onions, peeled and quartered
2 cloves garlic, crushed
150ml/$^1/_4$ pint red wine
2-3 tablespoons brandy
1 level teaspoon dried thyme
$^1/_4$ level teaspoon ground coriander
Good pinch of celery salt
Salt and pepper
2 fresh bay leaves
To garnish:
Slices of hard-boiled egg
Gherkins

Coarsely mince (or chop in a food processor) the raw goose meat, pork fat, bacon, goose liver and onions. Mix well with the garlic, wine, brandy, thyme, coriander, celery salt and plenty of seasonings.

Grease 900g/2lb loaf tin and place the bay leaves in the base. Spoon the pâté mixture on top, pressing down evenly. Stand in a roasting tin containing 4cm/1$^1/_2$in water and bake in a moderate oven (160°C/325°F, Gas Mark 3) for about 2 hours or until the juices run clear when pierced with a skewer. Remove from water bath, cool under a weighted plate, then chill overnight.

To serve, turn out carefully and garnish with slices of hard-boiled egg and gherkin fans.
SERVES 8-10

Note: suitable to freeze for 6-8 weeks

WILD GOOSE PÂTÉ

VENISON
A HEALTHY CHOICE

THERE are seven species of deer in this country but really only three which are regularly eaten as venison. These are the red deer, fallow deer and roe deer. The red deer is the largest and said by some sources to be the only deer meat which should correctly be called venison. However, all deer meat is known as venison whether correct or not. There are two smaller deer called muntjac and sika and these are sometimes eaten when they are available.

All venison lacks natural fat so when roasted it must have tremendous help to keep it moist and tender. Very young animals may be roasted, almost unhung and unmarinated, but with most venison it is advisable to hang thoroughly – as with beef and other meats – to bring out the true flavour and encourage tenderness. Everyone knows that fresh, bright-red beef will not be as good as a side or joint which has been well hung and become a deep, dark reddish-brown, and the same applies to venison, if not more so. Hanging should be for up to 2 weeks.

The meat of the red deer is said to be superior to that of fallow and roe. The red has the strongest and best flavour. It needs more hanging than other types, but the roe deer, being smaller, is generally more tender and requires less hanging. The fallow deer is said to come between the two for flavour and has a more delicate taste. It is also likely to be more tender than the others. If you have a chance to try the two small species of deer, the flavour is good and on the whole tender.

The open season for shooting deer varies from species to species and also from male to female. Red deer males are called stags and the females hinds while those of the fallow and roe are known as bucks and does respectively. Buck or stag venison is usually considered superior to that of the doe or hind, but this is a matter of preference. The best roasting joint is the haunch or saddle, but the loin and fillet may also be roasted and loin chops make excellent barbecue food as does a small haunch if wrapped securely in foil for the majority of the cooking time.

Steaks and chops fry beautifully but use more fat than you would for beef steaks. It is the liver which is the great delicacy and is usually considered one of the stalker's perks. It is removed from the animal as soon as it is killed and eaten as soon as possible, usually simply fried in butter; but it also makes a quite delicious pâté if you are able to get hold of even a small quantity. Venison is becoming easier to obtain for some country butchers have found regular suppliers, and the game shops tend to have good supplies. Also the many deer farms provide an outlet for obtaining good venison and venison sausages. All over the country deer farms are springing up to meet the new demand for venison, and as the availability improves over the next few years we hope the prices will also begin to drop.

Venison not only freezes very well but even seems to improve with freezing. The lack of fat prevents it turning rancid during the freezing process and indeed one of the best haunches we ever tasted had been in the freezer for over three years. Venison is an excellent source of protein at a low calorific value.

VENISON PASTA SALAD
(pictured opposite, recipe on page 77)

Venison recipes

BASIC ROAST VENISON

The best joints to roast are the saddle, haunch or loin of venison. The haunch or loin may be roasted on the bone or be boned and rolled with stuffing added if liked. Remember all venison is virtually fat-free so it needs plenty of added fat both as fatty bacon rashers or slices of pork fat laid over the joint and plenty of dripping or oil to cook in.

Roast either after marinating for 24-48 hours in a marinade of red or white wine, cider or wine vinegar with added onion, garlic (if liked), cloves and other herbs: or, if known to be young and tender (say under 18 months old), then the marinade may be omitted.

The joint may either be wrapped in foil or left as it is or be pot-roasted with the addition of wine, cider or stock to the roasting tin, with the lid or covering removed for the last 30 minutes or so of cooking. The recipes for Roast Venison with Cranberry Stuffing and Venison en Croute give details for roasting.

A stuffed joint or haunch on the bone wrapped in foil should be cooked in a hot oven (220ºC/425ºF, Gas Mark 7) allowing 25-30 minutes per 450g/1lb with the foil folded back for the last 30 minutes or so. Without foil, joints including a saddle should be cooked in a fairly hot oven (200ºC/400ºF, Gas Mark 6) allowing about 30 minutes per 450g/1lb with plenty of basting. These times have to be adjusted slightly according to the sizes and types of joint, depending on which type of deer it is from.

Traditional accompaniments for roast venison are a thickish brown gravy flavoured with port or wine and possibly orange; or a Cumberland sauce, and redcurrant jelly, cranberry or gooseberry jelly or sauce, and possibly braised chestnuts, or sprouts with chestnuts and braised celery.

VENISON AND HAZELNUT CRUMBLE

A crunchy nut and wholemeal flour topping makes an interesting contrast to the spicy cubes of venison.

900g/2lb stewing venison
2-3 tablespoons oil
2-3 leeks, trimmed, sliced, washed and drained
1 level tablespoon ground coriander
100g/4oz mushrooms, quartered
1 1/2 level tablespoons flour
300ml/1/2 pint venison or beef stock
Salt and pepper
Hazelnut Crumble:
75g/3oz hazelnut kernels
100g/4oz wholemeal flour
2 level teaspoons ground coriander
50g/2oz butter or margarine

Cut the venison into cubes and fry in the heated oil until sealed. Transfer to a casserole. Add the leeks and coriander to the pan and fry gently for 2-3 minutes.

Add the mushrooms and continue for a minute or so longer. Sprinkle on the flour, mix in and then gradually add the stock.

Bring up to the boil, season well and pour over the venison. Cover and cook in a moderate oven (160ºC/325ºF, Gas Mark 3) for 1 1/4-1 1/2 hours or until almost tender; adjust the seasonings. Increase the oven temperature to fairly hot (200ºC/400ºF, Gas Mark 6).

For the crumble: mix together with

BASIC ROAST VENISON

VENISON AND HAZLENUT CRUMBLE

hazelnuts, flour and coriander and rub in the fat. Season well and spoon over the venison. Return to the oven, uncovered, and cook for about 30 minutes or until well browned. Serve hot.
SERVES 5-6

Note: suitable to freeze without the crumble for up to a month.

VENISON PASTA SALAD
(pictured on page 74)

A good way to use up the left-overs of a venison joint. The dressing will prevent the meat from becoming dry.

225g/8oz cooked venison, cut into thin strips
350g/12oz pasta spirals or macaroni
Salt and pepper
5 sticks celery, thinly sliced
1 red pepper, deseeded, sliced and blanched
300g/11oz can sweetcorn kernels, drained
1 bunch spring onions, trimmed and sliced
100g/4oz button mushrooms, trimmed and sliced
1-2 courgettes, trimmed and very thinly sliced
6 tablespoons French dressing

Cook the pasta in plenty of boiling salted water until just tender; then drain and refresh in cold water. Place in a bowl with the celery, pepper, sweetcorn, onions, mushrooms and courgettes. Mix the dressing with the venison and season well. Add to the salad and toss thoroughly.

Turn into a salad bowl and serve with crusty bread.
SERVES 4-5

POT ROAST VENISON WITH LENTILS

The lentils not only give a splendid flavour to the venison but help to keep it very moist, too.

Haunch of venison, boned and rolled (approx 1.8kg/4lb)
8-10 streaky bacon rashers
4 tablespoons oil
12 button onions, peeled and halved
2.5cm/1in piece fresh ginger, peeled and grated
1 clove garlic, crushed
150ml/¼ pint red wine
300ml/½ pint stock
2 bay leaves
8 whole cloves
¼ level teaspoon ground allspice
Salt and pepper
175g/6oz red lentils
To garnish:
Watercress

Wrap the bacon rashers around the venison. Heat the oil in a pan and fry the joint all over until well sealed – about 10 minutes. Remove from the pan. Add the onions, ginger and garlic to the pan and fry gently until lightly browned. Add the wine and stock and bring to the boil; add the bay leaves, cloves, allspice and seasonings.

Lay the lentils in the base of a casserole and put the venison on top. Pour the onion and stock mixture overall and cover tightly.

Cook in a moderate oven (180°C/350°F, Gas Mark 4) for about 2 hours, until tender. Discard the bay leaves and cloves and serve the venison in slices with the lentil sauce garnished with watercress.
SERVES 6-8

VENISON PASTA SALAD

POT ROAST VENISON WITH LENTILS

Venison recipes

VENISON EN CROUTE

This is my favourite way of serving a joint of venison.

2.25-2.75kg/5-6lb haunch of venison
1 onion peeled and chopped
1 bay leaf
175g/6oz streaky bacon rashers derinded
Salt and pepper
4-5 tablespoons oil or dripping
3 level tablespoons flour
5-6 tablespoons port
3 level tablespoons redcurrant, cranberry or japonica jelly
2-3 teaspoons lemon juice
Stuffing:
40g/1½oz butter or margarine
1 onion, peeled and chopped
175g/6oz mushrooms chopped
40g/1½oz fresh breadcrumbs
1 level teaspoon French mustard
⅔ teaspoon dried thyme
Pastry:
450g/1lb puff pastry
Beaten egg to glaze
To garnish:
Watercress

VENISON EN CROUTE
(pictured below)

Bone the venison and make stock with the bones, 1.2-1.75 litres/2-3 pints water, the onion and bay leaf. The boned joint should weigh around 1.75kg/4lb. Roll the meat into a neat joint, arrange the bacon rashers around it and secure with string. Season well and spread all over with dripping or oil. Roast in a fairly hot oven (200°C/400°F, Gas Mark 6) for 1¼-1½ hours, basting several times. Remove to a plate and leave until cold.

Spoon off excess fat from the drippings, then stir the flour into the residue. Cook for 2-3 minutes then gradually add 900ml/1½ pints of the stock and bring to the boil, stirring frequently. Add the port, jelly, lemon juice and seasonings and boil until reduced to about 600ml/1 pint. Leave to cool.

For the stuffing, melt the fat in a pan and fry the onion gently until soft. Add the mushrooms and continue for a minute or so. Remove from the heat, stir in the breadcrumbs, mustard, herbs and seasonings and leave to cool. When the venison is cold, roll out the pastry to a rectangle large enough to enclose the joint and spread the mushroom stuffing over the centre of the pastry.

Place the joint in the centre, after removing the string, and enclose in the pastry, sealing the edges with water. Place in a lightly greased roasting tin with the pastry joins underneath. Glaze all over with beaten egg. Use the pastry trimmings to decorate with a flower and leaf design. Glaze design.

At this stage the dish can be kept in a cool place for several hours before proceeding. Before baking, glaze again and then cook in a fairly hot oven (200°C/400°F, Gas Mark 6) for 30 minutes. Reduce the temperature to moderate (180°C/350°F, Gas Mark 4), lay a sheet of greaseproof paper over the pastry and cook for a further hour. To serve, reheat the sauce and bring to the boil for a few minutes. Transfer to a sauce boat. Place the venison on a large plate or board and garnish with watercress. Serve in fairly thick slices. SERVES 8

VENISON STEAKS WITH GHERKINS

A quick and easy recipe with a tangy slightly creamy sauce.

4 venison steaks
Salt and coarsely ground black pepper
40g/1¹/₂oz butter or margarine
1 tablespoon oil
1 clove garlic, crushed
1 level tablespoon very finely chopped onion
4 level tablespoons chopped gherkins
2 tablespoons Marsala or sherry
1 tablespoon lemon juice

3-4 tablespoons cream, single or double
To garnish:
Freshly chopped parsley

Season the steaks lightly with salt and quite generously with coarse pepper. Heat the fat and oil in a frying pan and when hot add the steaks.

Brown quickly on each side to seal in the juices and then lower the heat a little and continue to cook for 2-4 minutes each side until cooked to your taste. Quickly remove the steaks from the pan and keep warm. Add the garlic and onion to the pan juices and fry quickly until lightly coloured.

Add the gherkins, Marsala and lemon juice and stir thoroughly over a gentle heat until bubbling. Add the cream, reheat gently and season. Spoon the sauce over the steaks, sprinkle with parsley and serve. SERVES 4

VENISON STEAKS WITH GHERKINS
(pictured below)

Venison recipes

VENISON SAUTÉ

This method of cooking venison is much quicker than most and gives an excellent result but the cut must be from the tender part of the animal. The marinating process is a matter of preference and probably time. The pieces of venison may also be cooked on a barbecue.

Loin or haunch of venison
Marinade
150ml/¼ pint oil
300ml/½ pint white wine
150ml/¼ pint white wine vinegar
or cider vinegar
or a flavoured wine vinegar
6 juniper berries, crushed
1 onion, peeled and sliced
1 clove garlic, crushed
Little grated orange rind
2 bay leaves, crushed
Salt and pepper
50g/2oz butter or margarine
2 tablespoons oil
Little lemon juice
To garnish
Lemon wedges and watercress

Cut the venison into neat slices approx 2cm/³/4in thick, allowing one slice per person. Place in a shallow dish. If using the marinade combine all the ingredients, pour over the venison, cover and leave in a cool place for 24 hours, turning once. If not marinating, simply rub the venison with a cut clove of garlic. Heat a large frying pan with the butter and oil in it. Drain the venison and fry gently on each side until browned, allowing about 10 minutes each side. Lower the heat, cover the pan and cook gently for a further 15-20 minutes or until tender. Arrange the slices of venison on a hot serving dish and keep warm. Spoon off any excess fat from the pan juices and strain the marinade into the pan. Bring to the boil and boil briskly for 3-4 minutes. Adjust seasonings, sharpen the sauce with lemon juice if necessary and spoon over the steaks.

Garnish with lemon and watercress.
SERVES 4-6

VENISON WITH GREEN PEPPERCORN SAUCE

A tangy sauce flavoured with green peppercorns, dillweed and redcurrant jelly to serve with a boned and rolled lean joint of venison.

1.5kg/3½ lb haunch or loin of
venison, boned and rolled
175g/6oz streaky bacon rashers
4-5 tablespoons oil
Salt and pepper
2 level tablespoons flour
3 level tablespoons redcurrant jelly
6 tablespoons port
150ml/¼ pint white wine
2 level tablespoons green
peppercorns (from a can or jar)
³/4 level teaspoon dried dillweed
Lemon juice (optional)
To garnish
Spring onion tassles
Bacon rolls

You can use the bones from the venison with a chopped onion, bay leaf and water to make a stock by simmering for about 2 hours. Drain and reserve about 450ml/³/4 pint (otherwise use a good stock).

Roll the venison into a neat joint and secure with string, if not already done; then lay the bacon evenly all over it.

Stand on a piece of foil and season well. Pour the oil overall and wrap up

VENISON SAUTÉ

VENISON WITH GREEN PEPPERCORN SAUCE

loosely to enclose. Stand in a baking tin and cook in a fairly hot oven (200°C/400°F, Gas Mark 6) allowing 35 minutes per 450g/1lb and open up the foil for the last 30 minutes of the cooking time. When ready, remove from the foil and keep warm.

Put 2-3 tablespoons of the fat and the juices from the venison into a saucepan with the flour and cook for a minute or so. Gradually add the stock, redcurrant jelly, port and wine and bring up to the boil.

Boil uncovered until reduced to about 450ml/3/4 pint. Strain into a clean pan and add the peppercorns, dillweed and seasoning to taste. Add a touch of lemon juice if liked. Reheat and simmer for 2-3 minutes.

Serve the venison in slices with some of the sauce spooned over the garnished with spring onions and bacon rolls. Serve the rest of the sauce in a jug.
SERVES 6

ROAST VENISON WITH CRANBERRY STUFFING

The slight tartness of the cranberries and texture of the walnuts blend beautifully with the rather rich flavour of venison and this makes a really good party dish.

**Haunch of venison
(approx 2.3-2.7g/5-6lb)
1 onion, peeled and chopped
25g/1oz butter and margarine
6 tablespoons oil
175g/6oz whole cranberries, fresh
or frozen
Salt and pepper
1/2 level teaspoon dried thyme
40g/11/2 oz shelled walnuts,
chopped**

**75g/3oz fresh breadcrumbs
10 streaky bacon rashers**
Sauce:
**1 level tablespoon flour
4 tablespoons red wine
200ml/7fl oz stock
1 level teaspoon tomato purée
Juice of 1 orange**
To garnish:
**Parsley
Orange slices**

For the stuffing, fry the onion gently in the melted fat and 2 tablespoons oil until soft. Add the cranberries and continue gently until they soften and 'pop' in a covered pan.

Turn into a bowl, add seasonings, thyme, walnuts and breadcrumbs and mix together lightly.

Use to stuff the joint and secure with skewers and/or string. Season the joint and wrap the bacon around it. Stand on a sheet of foil, pour the remaining oil over and close the foil. Stand in a roasting tin and cook in a hot oven (220°C/425°F, Gas Mark 7) allowing about 25-30 minutes per 450g/1lb.

Fold back the foil for the last 30 minutes and baste several times.

Pour the cooking juices into a pan, spoon off excess fat then stir in the flour and cook for a minute or so.

Gradually add the wine and stock and bring up to the boil. Add tomato purée and orange juice, season well and simmer for 3-4 minutes; strain into a jug.

Serve the venison (still with the bacon rashers in place, if liked) and garnish with parsley and orange slices and with the sauce served separately.
SERVES 6-8

ROAST VENISON WITH CRANBERRY STUFFING

Venison recipes

ROAST VENISON WITH CRANBERRY PEARS

This dish is enhanced by the sweetness of the pears and slight tartness of the cranberry filling.

1.3kg/3lb loin of venison, boned and rolled
Marinade
1 carrot, peeled and sliced
1 onion, peeled and chopped
1 stick celery, chopped
6 black peppercorns
1 bouquet garni
450ml/^{3}/4 pint red wine
To garnish:
2 level teaspoons powdered gelatine
6 tablespoons very hot water
8 level tablespoons cranberry sauce
8 pear halves, canned or fresh

Mix together all the marinade ingredients. Place the venison in a large dish and pour the marinade over it. Cover and leave to marinate in the refrigerator overnight or for at least 8 hours. Turn the joint occasionally. Drain the venison and place on a large piece of foil in a roasting tin. Strain the marinade and pour 150ml/^{1}/4 pint over the meat. Seal the foil loosely around the joint and cook in a moderately hot oven (190°C/375°F, Gas Mark 5) allowing 35 minutes per 450g/1lb. Open up the foil for the last 30 minutes of cooking time to allow the meat to brown.

Meanwhile dissolve the gelatine in the water, add to the cranberry sauce and mix well. Chill for about an hour or until set. Break up the jelly gently with a fork and use to fill the hollows in the pear halves left by the removal of the core. To serve, put the hot, roast venison on a serving dish and surround with the pear halves. The cooking juices may be mixed with the remainder of the marinade and thickened with a little cornflour blended with cold water. Bring back to the boil, adjust seasonings and serve in a sauce boat.
SERVES 8

VENISON CASSEROLE

Joints which you are little uncertain about can be used satisfactorily here. Cut the flesh from the bones into 2.5-5cm/1-2in cubes and use the bones to make stock.

900g/2lb shoulder of venison (or other cut)
^{1}/2 bottle red wine
2 carrots, peeled and sliced
4 whole cloves
Few whole black peppercorns
1 large onion, peeled and sliced
1 bay leaf
350g/12 oz button onions, peeled
175g/6 oz streaky bacon rashers, derinded and chopped
1 tablespoon oil or dripping
25g/1oz butter or margarine
600ml/1 pint stock
Salt and pepper
Little cornflour
To garnish:
Fried bread triangles
Lemon slices and chopped parsley

Put the cubed venison in a bowl with the wine, carrots, cloves, peppercorns, onion and bay leaf and leave to stand for 2-4 hours or longer if convenient. Fry the button onions and bacon in the oil and butter until lightly browned; transfer to a casserole. Drain

ROAST VENISON WITH CRANBERRY PEARS

VENISON CASSEROLE

the venison and fry in the same fat until sealed. Transfer to the casserole and strain in the marinade. Bring the stock to the boil, season well and pour over the venison. Cover tightly and cook in a very moderate oven (160°C/325°F, Gas Mark 3) for about 2¹/2 hours or until tender. Discard the bay leaf and thicken the sauce with the cornflour blended in a little cold water. Bring back to the boil, adjust seasonings and serve garnished with triangles of fried bread and lemon slices dipped in chopped parsley. SERVES 6

SPICED VENISON

Based on an Australian method, the spices and vinegar give an amazing flavour and tenderness to the venison.

1/2 level teaspoon grated nutmeg
1/2 level teaspoon ground cinnamon
1.5-1.8kg/3 ¹/2-4lb boned joint of venison, rolled
12 whole cloves
1 large onion, peeled and thinly sliced
2 cloves garlic, crushed
100g/4oz soft brown sugar
150ml/¹/4 pint wine vinegar
Salt and pepper
150ml/¹/4 pint water
1 level tablespoon cornflour
To garnish:
Courgette slices
Small broccoli spears

Combine the spices and rub all over the piece of venison. Stand in a casserole or dish. Add the cloves, onion and garlic to the casserole then blend the sugar, vinegar, salt, pepper and water together and pour over the venison. Cover tightly and leave in a cold place (preferably the refrigerator) for 24-36 hours, turning the venison several times so it is well marinated.

When ready to cook, turn the venison once more, cover tightly and cook in a moderate oven (180°C/350°F, Gas Mark 4) for about 2 hours until tender, basting twice. Remove the venison to a serving dish and keep warm. Discard the cloves from the juices. Blend the cornflour in a little cold water, add to the juices and bring back to the boil for 2-3 minutes. If too thick add a little more water, then adjust seasonings and serve with the venison which should be garnished with courgettes and broccoli. Carve the joint in thick slices for this recipe. SERVES 5-6

Note: this is excellent served cold when it should be sliced thinly.

SPICED VENISON

Venison recipes

VENISON CASSEROLE WITH APRICOTS

This is a very good casserole to serve a large party of up to 12 people.

2.3kg/5lb venison, suitable for casseroling
100g/4oz butter or margarine
3-4 tablespoons oil
4 large onions, peeled and sliced
3-4 cloves garlic, crushed
5 level tablespoons flour
3 level tablespoons tomato purée
600ml/1 pint red wine
600ml/1 pint stock
185g/6¹/₂oz jar cranberry sauce
350g/12oz no-need-to-soak dried apricots, halved
100g/4oz raisins
Salt and pepper
2 tablespoons lemon juice
4-6 tablespoons brandy
¹/₂ level teaspoon ground allspice
2 x 200g/7oz can water chestnuts, drained and sliced
1 bouquet garni

Cut the venison into cubes, discarding any sinews or fat, approx 2.5-4cm/1-1¹/₂in. Heat some of the fat and oil in a pan and fry the venison cubes, a few at a time to seal thoroughly. Transfer to a large casserole. Add more fat and oil as necessary, and then add the onions and garlic to the pan. Fry gently stirring frequently until beginning to brown. Stir in the flour and tomato purée and cook for a minute or so and then gradually add the wine and stock and bring to the boil, stirring occasionally. Add the cranberry sauce, apricots, raisins and seasonings and heat gently until the sauce has melted, then add the lemon juice, brandy, allspice, water chestnuts and bouquet garni. Pour into the casserole, cover and cook in a moderate oven (180°C/ 350°F, Gas Mark 4) for about 2¹/₂ hours or until tender. If the sauce is too thick, add a little boiling water, stir well, adjust the seasonings and serve.
SERVES 12

MEDALLIONS OF VENISON WITH MUSTARD CREAM SAUCE

Take care not to overcook the fillet of venison or keep it hot for long.

675g/1¹/₂lb venison fillet, cut into 8 slices
Salt and pepper
1 clove garlic, crushed
25g/1oz butter
1 tablespoon oil
2 level teaspoons French mustard
1 level teaspoon made English mustard
2 level teaspoons flour
200ml/7fl oz medium or dry cider
100g/4oz button mushrooms, sliced
4 tablespoons soured cream or natural yoghurt
To garnish:
Strips of green pepper

Season the medallions of venison and rub lightly with crushed garlic. Melt the butter and oil in a pan and fry the venison until well sealed and browned on both sides, but not overcooked. Remove from the pan and keep warm. Stir the mustards into the pan juices followed by the flour and cook for a minute or so. Gradually add the cider and bring up to the boil. Simmer for 2-3 minutes then add the mushrooms and simmer for a further 2-3 minutes. Stir in the soured cream or yoghurt and season to taste. Bring

lowly back to the boil. Spoon the sauce onto a serving dish and arrange the medallions in a line down the centre of the plate or divide between four dinner plates and arrange them attractively. Garnish with strips of green pepper and serve.
SERVES 4

VENISON CARBONNADE

A good beery stew for a cold day.

900g/2lb venison, cut into
5cm/2in pieces
1 tablespoon oil
25g/1oz butter or margarine
2 onions, peeled and sliced
2 cloves garlic, crushed
2 level tablespoons flour
300ml/1/2 pint brown ale
300ml/1/2 pint good stock
3 bay leaves
10 whole cloves
3 tablespoons wine vinegar
2 level tablespoons brown sugar
1 level tablespoon tomato purée
Salt and black pepper
4 carrots, peeled and sliced
100-175g/4-6oz tiny button
mushrooms
To garnish:
Freshly chopped herbs

Heat the oil and fat in a pan and fry the pieces of venison until well sealed; transfer to a casserole. Fry the onions and garlic in the same fat until soft then stir in the flour and cook for a minute or so. Gradually add the ale and stock and bring up to the boil. Add the bay leaves, cloves, vinegar, sugar, tomato purée, seasonings and carrots and pour over the venison. Cover tightly and cook in a moderate oven (180°C/350°F, Gas Mark 4) for 1¹/2 hours. Add the mushrooms, stir well and return to the oven for 15 minutes. Discard the bay leaves and cloves and serve with the fresh herbs.
SERVES 5-6

POTTED VENISON

Little mousses of cooked venison set in individual moulds.

225g/8oz cooked venison
4 level tablespoons cranberry sauce
1 tablespoon port
2 tablespoons water
2 teaspoons lemon juice
15g/1/2oz packet powdered gelatine
275ml/scant 1/2 pint clear brown
stock
Salt and pepper
To garnish:
Watercress

Put the cranberry sauce, port, water and lemon juice into a saucepan and heat gently, but do not boil. Sprinkle over 1 level teaspoon of the gelatine and stir until dissolved. Divide the mixture between four lightly greased 100-150ml/4-5fl oz moulds or dishes. Chill for about 30 minutes or until set.

Dissolve the remaining 2 level teaspoons gelatine in the very hot – not boiling – stock, season well and allow to cool slightly. Roughly chop or coarsely mince the venison and fill the four moulds, dividing the meat equally between them. Gently pour the dissolved gelatine over the venison to fill the moulds. Cool and then chill for at least 2 hours or until set. To serve, turn out the potted venison by dipping quickly into hot water and then turn out onto one large or four individual dishes.
SERVES 4

VENISON
CARBONNADE

POTTED VENISON

RABBIT
ABUNDANT 'GAME'

RABBITS are not classified as game, but no game cookery book would really be complete without mention of them. Rabbits can be shot at any time of the year and are at their best aged between three and four months old. They are on the increase again as myxomatosis appears to have lost the stronghold which it once had, although small outbreaks do occur quite frequently but no longer spread as they once used to. More rabbits now live above ground rather than in deep burrows where the disease spread like wildfire and this may well account for part of the increase.

A young rabbit should be plump with bright eyes, flexible feet and smooth claws. The ears of a young rabbit will tear easily. Rabbits must be paunched as soon as possible after killing and before hanging. Some people will paunch them on the spot, as they are shot. Hang for 3-4 days, head downwards, before skinning, cleaning and cooking. If you don't want to hang them, they are easier to skin while still warm.

The wild rabbit has a much better flavour than those specially bred for the table or the frozen varieties from China and other countries.

Rabbits are widely available fresh from butchers and poulterers as well as from farm shop outlets and gamedealers. They also come frozen, whole, in portions, chopped or boned, from butchers and supermarkets. Rabbit is a fairly cheap meat to buy but is very tasty and well worth a try. It is almost fat free so is an excellent source of protein that is low in calories. Generally use only young rabbits for roasting and keep the more mature ones for braising and stews.

BASIC ROAST RABBIT

1 young rabbit, prepared
1 onion, peeled and minced
2 tablespoons oil
100g/4oz fresh white breadcrumbs
2 level teaspoons dried thyme
3 level tablespoons freshly chopped parsley
Salt and pepper
25g/1oz shelled walnuts, chopped
1 dessert apple, peeled, cored and coarsely grated
1 egg, beaten
225g/8oz streaky bacon rashers, derinded
75g/3oz dripping or margarine
8 medium onions, peeled

Wash and dry the rabbit thoroughly. Fry the minced onions in the oil until soft and lightly browned. Add the breadcrumbs, herbs, seasonings, walnuts and apple. Mix well together then bind with the egg. Use to stuff the rabbit, close up with skewers or sew up loosely. Place the bacon over the back of the rabbit and tie loosely with string, if necessary. Stand in a well-greased roasting tin and pour the dripping or fat over the rabbit. Season lightly and place the onions around the rabbit. Roast in a fairly hot oven (200°C/400°F, Gas Mark 6) for about an hour, basting every 15 minutes. If liked, remove the bacon from the rabbit, dredge lightly with flour and return to the oven for 10-20 minutes or until well browned and cooked through. Serve on a warmed dish surrounded with baked onions and use the pan juices to make a gravy. Serve with a sharp sauce such as cranberry or japonica jelly.
SERVES 4-5 (*See note over*)

RABBIT WITH APRICOT AND ORANGE SAUCE (*pictured opposite, recipe on page 94*)

BASIC ROAST RABBIT

Rabbit recipes

Note: the rabbit may also be pot-roasted with 300ml/^{1}/$_2$ pint stock or a mixture of stock and white wine or cider added to the pan and the rabbit covered with foil for the first 45 minutes of the cooking time. An extra 15 minutes or so will be required to complete the cooking.

POACHER'S STEW WITH DUMPLINGS

A good old-fashioned style stewed rabbit, served with bacon and herb dumplings.

900g/2lb rabbit, cut into 8 pieces
25g/1oz lard or margarine
1 large onion, peeled and chopped
2 sticks celery, chopped
25g/1oz flour
300ml/^{1}/$_2$ pint brown ale
300ml/^{1}/$_2$ pint stock
Salt and pepper
Dumplings:
4 rashers streaky bacon, derinded
100g/4oz self-raising flour
Pinch of salt
40g/1^1/$_2$oz shredded suet
1 level tablespoon freshly chopped parsley
^{3}/$_4$ level teaspoon dried thyme
3-4 tablespoons cold water

Heat the fat in a large pan and fry the onion and celery gently for 5 minutes. Coat the rabbit in the flour and add to the pan. Fry for 5 minutes or so, turning frequently until lightly browned. Add the beer and stock and bring to the boil, stirring occasionally. Season, reduce the heat, cover and simmer gently for an hour.

For the dumplings, fry the bacon until crisp then cool slightly and chop finely. Sift together the flour and salt, add suet, herbs and bacon and mix to a soft dough with water. Shape into 8 balls and add to the pan with the rabbit and continue to simmer for 20-25 minutes until the dumplings are risen and cooked.

Adjust the seasonings if necessary and serve at once.
SERVES 4

COUNTRY RABBIT PIE

A rabbit, leek and mushroom mixture layered in a pie dish and topped with shortcrust pastry. Ideally served hot, but also good served cold.

675g/1^1/$_2$lb rabbit joints
25g/1oz lard or margarine
2 medium leeks, trimmed and sliced
25g/1oz flour
600ml/1 pint chicken stock
Grated rind of 1 lemon
100g/4oz mushrooms, quartered
2 carrots, peeled and sliced
Salt and pepper
Stuffing:
50g/2oz butter or margarine
50g/2oz streaky bacon, derinded and finely chopped
1 onion, peeled and finely chopped
2 sticks celery, finely chopped
3 level tablespoons freshly chopped parsley
100g/4oz fresh white breadcrumbs
Pastry:
225g/8oz plain flour
^{1}/$_2$ level teaspoon salt
50g/2oz butter or margarine
50g/2oz lard or white fat
Cold water to mix
Beaten egg or milk to glaze

Melt the fat in a large frying pan, add the rabbit joints and fry on both sides until browned, about 7-10 minutes. Remove the rabbit; add the leeks and fry for 2-3 minutes. Stir in the flour and cook for 1 minute then gradually add the stock and bring to the boil. Add lemon rind, mushrooms, carrots and seasonings and simmer for 5 minutes.

For the stuffing, melt the fat in a pan and fry bacon, onion and celery for 5-6 minutes. Remove from the heat and add parsley, breadcrumbs and seasonings and mix well. Form into 12 even-sized balls. Layer rabbit joints and stuffing balls in a pie dish and pour over the sauce. Leave to cool.

For the pastry, mix together the flour and salt, rub in the fats until the mixture resembles fine breadcrumbs, then add sufficient cold water to mix to a firm but pliable dough.

Knead lightly until smooth then roll out to about 5cm/2in larger than the top of the dish. Cut off a 2.5cm/1 in strip from the edge of the pastry and place around the dampened rim of the dish. Damp the pastry and cover with the pastry lid. Seal, trim, knock up and flute the edges; roll out pastry trimmings and cut out leaves to decorate the top.

Brush with beaten egg or milk and bake in a fairly hot oven (200ºC/400ºF, Gas Mark 6) for 1 hour. Cover the top with foil when the pastry is sufficiently browned.

Serve hot.

SERVES 4-6

CITRUS RABBIT

Joints of rabbit casseroled with white wine and grapefruit juice.

1 rabbit, jointed
50g/2oz plain flour
Salt and pepper
40g/1¹/₂oz butter or margarine
300ml/¹/₂ pint chicken stock
150ml/¹/₄ pint white wine
1 bouquet garni
150ml/¹/₄ pint grapefruit juice
200g/7oz can water chestnuts, drained and sliced (optional)
To garnish:
Freshly chopped parsley
Fried triangles of bread

Sift 25g/1oz flour with ¹/₂ level teaspoon salt and a pinch of pepper and dip the rabbit joints in this seasoned flour. Melt 25g/1oz fat in a frying pan, add the rabbit and fry lightly to brown the meat all over.

Transfer to an ovenproof casserole and pour over the stock and wine.

Add the bouquet garni and seasonings, cover the casserole and bake in a moderate oven (180ºC/350ºF, Gas Mark 4) for 1¹/₂ hours. Meanwhile, cream the remaining flour with the remaining fat.

Lift the rabbit onto a serving dish and keep warm. Strain the liquor into a small pan and boil hard until reduced to 300ml/¹/₂ pint.

Add the grapefruit juice and heat to almost boiling and then gradually whisk in knobs of butter and flour mixture.

Add the water chestnuts, if used, and simmer for 5 minutes. Adjust the seasonings and pour the sauce back over the rabbit.

Sprinkle with chopped parsley and surround with fried bread triangles. Serve at once.

SERVES 4

CITRUS RABBIT

Rabbit recipes

RABBIT SAUTÉ WITH MUSHROOMS

The orange marmalade and apricots add a tangy flavour to this dish.

1 young rabbit
Salt and pepper
2-3 tablespoons oil
150ml/^{1}/4 pint white wine
150ml/^{1}/4 pint stock
50-75g/2-3oz dried apricots, chopped
Grated rind and juice of 1 orange
2 level tablespoons coarse orange marmalade
100g/4oz mushrooms, quartered
2 tablespoons brandy (optional)
To garnish:
Chopped parsley
Wedges of orange

Trim the rabbit and strip the meat off the bones and cut into strips.

Heat the fat in a pan and fry the pieces gently until sealed all over.

Pour off all the fat from the pan and add the wine, stock, apricots, orange rind and juice, and marmalade.

Heat gently until melted then bring up to the boil and cover.

Simmer for about 25 minutes or until tender then add the mushrooms and brandy (if used) and continue for 5 minutes.

Adjust the seasonings and serve sprinkled with chopped parsley and with wedges of orange.
SERVES 4

RABBIT AND FENNEL HOTPOT

A hotpot is a dish baked in the oven with a topping of sliced potatoes. For this one the filling is layers of rabbit, onion and Florence fennel.

1 young rabbit (approx 900g/2lb), jointed
Approx 25g/1oz seasoned flour
350g/12oz onions, peeled and thinly sliced
1 large bulb Florence fennel, trimmed and chopped
675g/1^1/2lb potatoes, peeled and thinly sliced
Salt and pepper
Ground or grated nutmeg
2 tablespoons wine vinegar
150ml/^{1}/4 pint stock
To garnish:
Chopped parsley

Wash the rabbit well in salted water. Cut into small joints and dry. Coat in the seasoned flour. Place half the onions and half the fennel and a thin layer of potatoes in the base of a large

RABBIT SAUTÉ WITH MUSHROOMS
(pictured below)

RABBIT AND FENNEL HOTPOT

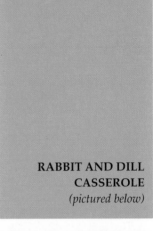

casserole. Cover with the pieces of rabbit and season well with salt, pepper and nutmeg. Cover with the remaining onions, fennel and finally sliced potatoes. Add the vinegar to the stock and pour into the casserole almost to cover the rabbit, adding a little more stock if necessary. Cover the casserole tightly and cook in a very moderate oven (160°C/325°F, Gas Mark 3) for about 2 hours.

Increase the cooking temperature to hot (220°C/425°F, Gas Mark 7), remove the lid from the casserole and continue for 15-20 minutes or until the potatoes are browned and crispy on top. Sprinkle with chopped parsley and serve.
SERVES 4

RABBIT AND DILL CASSEROLE
The flavour of dill, tomatoes and capers blend well with the rabbit.

675g/1¹/2lb small rabbit joints
2 tablespoons oil
2 onions, peeled and sliced
2 carrots, peeled and sliced
1 level tablespoon flour
450ml/³/4 pint stock
2 level tablespoons tomato purée
2 tablespoons wine vinegar
1 level tablespoon brown sugar
¹/2 teaspoon Worcestershire sauce
Salt and pepper
1 level tablespoon freshly chopped dill or 1-1¹/2 level teaspoons dried dillweed
1 level tablespoon capers

Cut the rabbit into even-sized pieces. Heat the oil in a pan and fry the rabbit until well sealed, then transfer to a large casserole. Fry the onions and carrots in the same fat for 2-3 minutes then add the flour and cook for 1 minute. Gradually add the stock, tomato purée, vinegar, sugar, Worcestershire sauce, plenty of seasonings and the dill and capers. Bring to the boil, simmer for 2 minutes then pour over the rabbit. Cover the casserole tightly and cook in a moderate oven (180°C/350°F, Gas Mark 4) for 1¹/4-1¹/2 hours until tender. Adjust the seasonings and serve with boiled rice or pasta. If desired 100g/4oz tiny button mushrooms may be added for the last 20 minutes of the cooking time.
SERVES 4-5

Note: Suitable to freeze for up to 2 months.

RABBIT AND DILL CASSEROLE
(pictured below)

Rabbit recipes

ELIZABETHAN RABBIT

Apples, raisins and artichokes as well as spices were often added to meat dishes in Elizabethan times and they do indeed give a new dimension to rabbit and game, as shown here. The recipe can also be used for hare and venison.

900g/2lb rabbit joints
25g/1oz flour
2 tablespoons oil
100g/4oz Jerusalem artichokes, peeled and sliced
175g/6oz onions, peeled and chopped
100g/4oz mushrooms, thickly sliced
100g/4oz carrots, peeled and chopped
250ml/8fl oz red wine
1 bouquet garni or 2 bay leaves
2 dessert apples, peeled, cored and roughly chopped
50g/2oz raisins
Grated rind and juice of 1 orange
Salt and pepper
300ml/1/2 pint stock
To garnish:
Freshly chopped parsley
Chopped garlic

Make sure the rabbit is jointed into at least 6 pieces and then coat with flour. Heat the oil in a pan and fry the rabbit until browned all over. Remove from the pan.

Fry the artichokes, onions, mushrooms and carrots until the onions are beginning to brown, then add the bouquet garni, apples, raisins, orange juice, seasonings and sufficient stock just to cover the rabbit.

Bring to the boil, cover and simmer very gently for about 2 hours or until the rabbit is very tender.

Taste and adjust the seasonings and serve sprinkled with the orange rind, chopped parsley and garlic; and with creamed potatoes.
SERVES 6

RABBIT AND APPLE FRICASSEE

Rabbit dishes have always been popular on the Continent and are now rapidly gaining favour here, especially as they are inexpensive and can be cooked in a wide variety of ways.

1 rabbit, prepared and jointed
2-3 level tablespoons flour
50g/2oz butter or margarine
4 rashers streaky bacon, derinded and chopped
1 large onion, peeled and sliced
2 sticks celery, sliced
2 cooking apples, peeled and sliced
300ml/1/2 pint milk
Approx 450ml/3/4 pint chicken stock
1 bay leaf
1 sprig fresh rosemary or thyme or 1 level teaspoon dried thyme
Salt and pepper
Lemon juice to taste
To garnish:
Apple rings
Little butter
Celery leaves

Coat the rabbit joints in flour and fry in the hot fat in a flameproof casserole until golden brown, turning once or twice. Remove from the casserole and fry the bacon, onion and celery until soft but not coloured, in the same fat.

Add the apples and cook for 2-3 minutes mixing well. Remove

ELIZABETHAN RABBIT

RABBIT AND APPLE FRICASSEE

casserole from the heat and stir in sufficient flour to absorb the fat – approx 1-2 tablespoons. Gradually blend in the milk and bring to the boil, stirring continuously. Replace the rabbit, then add sufficient stock barely to cover the joints. Add the herbs and seasonings, cover and simmer gently on the hob or cook in a moderate oven (160°C/325°F, Gas Mark 3) for an hour until the meat is tender.

When cooked discard bay leaf and sprigs of herbs and, if the sauce appears rather thin, strain it into a saucepan and boil until reduced and thickened, keeping the rabbit covered and warm; adjust seasoning and add lemon juice to taste. Pour back over the rabbit.

Garnish with the apple rings fried lightly in butter and with celery leaves.
SERVES 4

Note: Suitable to freeze for up to 2 months.

RABBIT AND MUSHROOM PIE

This is more of a puff pastry, square vol-au-vent with a rabbit, mushroom and green pepper filling. It tastes delicious and looks attractive too.

675g/1¹/₂lb rabbit joints
600ml/1 pint chicken stock
1 bay leaf
1 small sprig of fresh rosemary
or ¹/₄ level teaspoon dried
rosemary, crumbled
Salt and pepper
450g/1lb puff pastry
1 egg, beaten
225g/8oz button mushrooms,
trimmed
65g/2¹/₂oz butter or margarine
1 small green pepper, deseeded
and thinly sliced
50g/2oz flour
300ml/¹/₂ pint milk

Place the rabbit joints in a pan with the stock, bay leaf, rosemary, salt and pepper. Bring to the boil, cover and simmer for about an hour or until the rabbit is tender.

Roll out the pastry on a floured surface to make two 20cm/8in squares. Place one on a baking sheet and brush with beaten egg. Cover with the second square and mark a 2.5cm/1in border all round with a sharp knife. Score a lattice pattern within the square. Brush with egg and bake in a hot oven (220°C/425°F, Gas Mark 7) for 25 minutes.

Remove the rabbit pieces and herbs from the stock and boil the stock hard until reduced to 275 ml/scant ¹/₂ pint. Remove the bones from the rabbit and cut into 1cm/¹/₂in cubes. Keep a few of the mushrooms whole for garnish and quarter the rest. Heat 40g/1¹/₂oz fat in a pan and fry all the mushrooms gently for 2-3 minutes; then remove from the pan.

Add the rest of the fat and sliced pepper to the pan and fry gently for 2 minutes. Stir in the flour, cook for 1 minute then gradually blend in the milk and rabbit stock.

Bring to the boil stirring all the time. Add the quartered mushrooms and rabbit; adjust the seasonings and heat thoroughly.

Place the pastry case on a hot serving dish, fill with the rabbit mixture, top with the pastry lid and garnish with reserved whole mushrooms.
SERVES 4

RABBIT AND
MUSHROOM PIE

Rabbit recipes

RABBIT PASTIES

This recipe needs only about 2 portions of rabbit to make a tasty meal, packed lunch or picnic idea. The pasties are good served hot or cold and will freeze satisfactorily for up to 2 months.

225g/8oz shortcrust pastry (made using 225g/8oz plain flour etc)
175g/6oz boneless rabbit meat
2 rashers streaky bacon, derinded and chopped
1 small onion, peeled and finely chopped
1 carrot, peeled and finely chopped
50g/2oz sultanas or raisins
1/2 level teaspoon dried thyme
Salt and pepper
Beaten egg or milk to glaze

Make up the pastry, wrap and chill. Mince or very finely chop the rabbit and mix with the bacon, onion, carrot, sultanas or raisins, thyme and seasonings.

Roll out the pastry and cut out 4-5 circles approx 18cm/7in in diameter. Divide the filling between the pastry, damp the edges and bring together at the top to form a pasty.

Press the edges firmly together and crimp. Stand on a lightly greased baking sheet and glaze with beaten egg or milk.

Cook in a fairly hot oven (200°C/400°F, Gas Mark 6) for about 25-35 minutes or until well browned.

Serve hot or cold.
MAKES 4-5

Note: Hare or venison meat may be used in place of rabbit for these pasties.

RABBIT WITH APRICOT AND ORANGE SAUCE

(pictured on page 86)

A tangy sauce in which joints of rabbit are cooked in a frying pan.

675-900g/1¹/2-2lb rabbit pieces on the bone
Salt and pepper
1 clove garlic, crushed
75g/3oz no-need-to-soak apricots, halved
75g/3oz no-need-to-soak prunes or black olives
200ml/7fl oz water or stock
Grated rind of 2 oranges
Juice of 2 oranges
150ml/¹/4 pint white wine
150ml/¹/4 pint stock
2 tablespoons oil
1 tablespoon honey or brown sugar
1 tablespoon wine vinegar
To garnish:
Orange slices or wedges
Watercress

Season the pieces of rabbit well and rub with garlic. If rather large, cut them into smaller pieces.

Poach the apricot pieces and prunes or olives in the water or stock for about 15 minutes or until tender, then add the orange rind and juice, wine and stock. Heat the oil in a large frying pan and brown the pieces of rabbit all over, then continue until partly cooked through.

Pour off any excess fat from the pan and add the apricot and orange mixture. Bring up to the boil, cover and simmer gently for about 20 minutes or until the rabbit is tender, basting from time to time.

Add the sugar and vinegar, adjust the seasonings and continue

RABBIT PASTIES

RABBIT WITH APRICOT AND ORANGE SAUCE

for 2-3 minutes. Serve hot garnished with orange and watercress.
SERVES 4

Note: The orange rind may be finely pared off with a potato peeler and cut into julienne strips instead of grating to give more shape to the sauce.

DIJON RABBIT

Mustard has always been a good flavouring for rabbit and when teamed up with light ale, it improves the flavour even more.

1 rabbit, jointed
1 level tablespoon flour
1 level tablespoon dry mustard
2 tablespoons oil
25g/1oz butter or margarine
1 large onion, peeled and sliced
150ml/¼ pint light ale
150ml/¼ pint stock
Salt and pepper
1 tablespoon wine vinegar
2 level tablespoons demerara sugar
1 red pepper, deseeded and sliced
1 level tablespoon Dijon mustard
Topping:
50g/2oz fresh breadcrumbs
2 tablespoons oil
50g/2oz butter or margarine
1 level tablespoon snipped chives
1 level tablespoon freshly chopped parsley

Wipe the rabbit all over, then toss in a mixture of the flour and dry mustard. Heat the oil in a pan and fry the pieces of rabbit until browned all over. Transfer to a casserole.

Add the butter to the pan and fry the onions until soft. Stir in the remaining flour and mustard and cook for a minute or so. Gradually add the light ale and stock and bring up to the boil. Season well, add vinegar, sugar, red pepper and Dijon mustard and pour over the rabbit.

Cover and cook in a moderate oven (180°C/350°F, Gas Mark 4) for about an hour or until tender.

Meanwhile fry the crumbs in a mixture of oil and butter until golden brown, stirring frequently and then mix with the chives and parsley.

Remove the lid from the rabbit, adjust the seasonings and sprinkle with the crumb mixture.

Serve at once.
SERVES 4-5

DIJON RABBIT
(pictured below)

Rabbit recipes

CURRIED RABBIT

Rabbit lends itself beautifully to being cooked with curry spices. It is very easy to use a ready-made curry mix but the flavour is much better if you use the individual spices.

1 rabbit, jointed or approx 900g/2lb rabbit pieces
Little seasoned flour
2-3 tablespoons oil
1 large onion, peeled and sliced
2 cloves garlic, crushed
1 level teaspoon ground coriander
1 level teaspoon ground cumin
1 level teaspoon turmeric
1 level teaspoon ground fenugreek
1 level teaspoon garam masala
2 level teaspoons paprika
1/4-1/2 level teaspoon chilli powder
600ml/1 pint stock or water
Salt and pepper
3-4 level tablespoons desiccated coconut (optional)
To serve:
Poppadoms
Sliced tomatoes with onions
Lime pickle
Freshly chopped coriander

Coat the pieces of rabbit in seasoned flour then fry in the heated oil until browned all over. Remove from the pan. Add the onion to the fat and fry for a few minutes until soft. Add all the spices and cook together gently for 3-4 minutes until soft.

Add the stock or water and bring up to the boil. Replace the pieces of rabbit, season and add the coconut (if used).

Cover and simmer gently for about 45 minutes or until tender. If you prefer a thicker sauce add 1-2 level teaspoons cornflour blended with a little cold water and simmer for a further 5 minutes until thickened.

Serve with freshly boiled rice or basmati rice and accompanied by poppadoms, sliced tomatoes with onions, lime pickle and sprinkled with freshly chopped coriander.
SERVES 4

Note: spiced dishes are best not frozen or only for a few weeks as the spices can turn musty during storage.

SWEET AND SOUR RABBIT

Rabbit is excellent served with a sweet and sour sauce, the lean meat being ideal for this type of dish.

900g/2lb rabbit joints
Salt and pepper
2 tablespoons oil
1 onion, peeled and thinly sliced
100g/4oz carrots, peeled and cut into sticks
200g/7oz can pineapple pieces in natural juice
2 tablespoons wine vinegar
2 level tablespoons brown sugar or clear honey
1 tablespoon lemon juice
2 level teaspoons tomato purée
1/2 teaspoon Worcestershire sauce
1 red pepper, deseeded and sliced
1 green pepper, deseeded and sliced
2 level teaspoons cornflour

Trim the pieces of rabbit and cut into even-sized pieces, season lightly. Heat the oil in a pan and fry the rabbit until lightly browned all over. Transfer to a casserole. Fry the onion and carrots in the same oil for 2-3 minutes, drain off any excess fat from the pan. Drain the pineapple and

CURRIED RABBIT

SWEET AND SOUR RABBIT

combine the juice with the vinegar, sugar, lemon juice, tomato purée and Worcestershire sauce; add to the pan and bring to the boil. Season well.

Lay the peppers over the rabbit, pour over the sauce and cover tightly. Cook in a moderately hot oven (190°C/375°F, Gas Mark 5) for 45 minutes or until tender. Alternatively place in a microwave set on maximum (100%) for 6 minutes; turn over and cook a further 5-6 minutes.

Remove the rabbit to a serving dish and keep warm.

Blend the cornflour with the minimum of cold water, add to the sauce and bring back to the boil, stirring continuously. Simmer for a few minutes until thickened, adjust the seasonings and pour back over the rabbit. Serve with boiled rice or jacket potatoes.
SERVES 4

Note: if liked the sugar may be increased to give a sweeter flavour to the dish.

RABBIT PIE WITH PRUNES
Rabbit and prunes are often served together; here they form the filling of a top-crust pie.

1 young rabbit (approx 900g/2lb)
225g/8oz collar bacon, derinded and chopped
450ml/³/₄ pint water or stock
1 large onion, peeled and chopped
2 carrots, peeled and chopped
1 bay leaf
Juice of ¹/₂ lemon
Salt and pepper
200g/7oz plain flour
1 level tablespoon freshly chopped parsley

12 prunes, soaked, or no-need-to-soak prunes
40g/1¹/₂oz margarine
40g/1¹/₂oz lard or white fat
Cold water to mix
Beaten egg or milk to glaze

Soak the rabbit in salted water for 2 hours then drain well. This process is not strictly necessary but some people think rabbit has a slightly strong flavour and this removes any trace. Place in a saucepan with the bacon, stock, onion, carrots, bay leaf, lemon juice and seasonings. Bring to the boil, cover and simmer for ³/₄-1 hour until tender. Remove rabbit and strip the meat from the bones. Blend 25g/1oz flour with a little cold water and whisk into the cooking liquor and bring to the boil. Adjust seasonings, stir in the parsley, cooked rabbit and prunes. Pour into a pie dish and cool.

For the pastry, sift remaining flour with a pinch of salt, rub in the fats until the mixture resembles fine breadcrumbs then add sufficient cold water to mix to a pliable dough. Roll out the pastry larger than the top of the dish and cut a 2.5cm/1in strip for the rim of the dish.

Damp the rim, position pastry strip then dampen the strip. Cover with the pastry lid, press edges firmly together and crimp. Decorate top with pastry trimmings cut into leaves and brush with egg or milk. Make a hole in the centre for steam to escape and cook in a fairly hot oven (200°C/400°F, Gas Mark 6) for 20 minutes or so. Reduce temperature to moderate (180°C/350°F, Gas Mark 4) and continue for a further 20-25 minutes. Serve hot.
SERVES 4-6

RABBIT PIE WITH PRUNES

HARE
FULL-BLOODED MEAT

THERE ARE two species of British hare – the brown and the blue or mountain. It is the brown hare which is the larger and better for eating. A full-grown hare should serve 6-8 people, but of course the size does vary a lot. Young hares are called leverets and they are also good to eat, but serve only 4-5 people.

A young hare should have small, white teeth, a smooth coat and soft ears which will tear easily – if they are tough to tear then it is a fair sign that the hare is mature. The claws should be well hidden beneath the fur. As the hare matures the claws become long and blunt and project beyond the paw and the teeth become yellow and irregular. White hairs appear in the muzzle and the coat looks grey.

The close season for selling hares is March 1 to July 31 although many farm shops and gamedealers may sell them frozen all the year.

Once shot, hares should be hung head downwards (with a polythene bag or small bowl below the muzzle to catch any blood) for about a week depending on the weather. Obviously warm conditions will spoil the hare if left too long. It should only then be paunched, skinned and cleaned ready for fairly prompt cooking. The blood which collects under the membrane in the ribs should be retained and used for thickening and flavouring gravies and sauces to serve with the hare, but add it at the end of the cooking time otherwise it will cause the sauce to curdle if allowed to boil. Young hares are best roasted and older ones jugged or casseroled in some way. Raw hare may be frozen whole or in pieces for up to a year. Cooked hare dishes will freeze for 2-3 months.

BASIC ROAST HARE

Traditionally hare is roasted unstuffed, but in this recipe it is cooked whole, complete with head and the whole of the cavity filled with a herb stuffing. Bacon or pork fat is necessary when roasting as the flesh is fat-free and therefore likely to dry out without added fat and regular basting.

1 hare, skinned and paunched
Stuffing
175g/6oz fresh breadcrumbs
Finely grated rind of 1 lemon or orange
50g/2oz shredded suet
1 onion, peeled and finely chopped
1 level tablespoon chopped chives
1 level tablespoon freshly chopped parsley
1 level teaspoon dried thyme
6 anchovy fillets, chopped
Salt and pepper
Juice of 1/2 orange
Beaten egg to bind
225g/1/2lb streaky bacon rashers
Dripping
Flour
450ml/3/4 pint stock
1 level tablespoon tomato purée
1 teaspoon Worcestershire sauce
1 clove garlic, crushed
2 level tablespoons orange marmalade

Wipe the hare inside and out. For the stuffing, combine the breadcrumbs, fruit rind, suet, onion, chives, parsley, thyme and anchovies. Season well, add the orange juice and sufficient egg to bind together. Use to stuff the hare and sew up the cavity or secure with skewers. Lay the rashers of bacon along the back of the hare.

continued over

JUGGED HARE
(pictured opposite, recipe on page 100)

BASIC ROAST HARE

Hare recipes

BASIC ROAST HARE *continued*

Heat about 100g/4oz dripping in a roasting tin, add the hare and baste. Cook in a fairly hot oven (200°C/400°F, Gas Mark 6) for about 2 hours, basting frequently until tender. Remove the bacon, dredge lightly with flour and return to the oven for a few minutes until browned. Remove the hare and keep warm. Spoon off most of the excess fat from the juice and stir 2 level tablespoons flour into the residue. Cook for a few minutes or until evenly browned, stirring continuously. Gradually add the stock, tomato purée, Worcestershire sauce, garlic and marmalade and bring up to the boil, stirring continously.

Simmer for 2-3 minutes, add a little more stock if too thick, then strain into a jug to serve with the hare. Garnish with fresh vegetables.
SERVES 6-8

BAKED HARE WITH CREAM SAUCE

Start this recipe the day before by marinating the joints in white wine. The final baking is simple and produces a tasty casserole.

1 young hare, prepared and jointed
300ml/1/2 pint dry white wine
4 tablespoons oil
3-4 fresh bay leaves
Salt and pepper
5-6 tablespoons double cream
To garnish:
Mini chipolata sausages
Fried cubes of bread
Stuffed olives

Put the joints of hare into a deep casserole. Mix the wine, oil, bay leaves and seasonings together and pour over the hare. Cover and leave to marinate for several hours, preferably for up to 24 hours, turning occasionally.

Cover the casserole and cook in a moderate oven (180°C/350°F, Gas Mark 4) for about 2 hours giving an occasional stir, until tender. Discard the bay leaves.

Pour off a little of the sauce and blend with the cream, then return it all to the casserole. Reheat gently, adjust the seasonings and serve garnished with chipolata sausages, fried cubes of bread and stuffed olives.
SERVES 4-6

JUGGED HARE *(pictured on page 98)*

One of the real classic dishes. It is not essential to add the hare's blood to the sauce although it improves the flavour; if it is added make sure the sauce is not reboiled or it will curdle.

1 hare, skinned and jointed
300ml/1/2 pint red wine
4 tablespoons oil
1/2 level teaspoon dried marjoram
1 onion, peeled and sliced
2 bay leaves
Few whole cloves
Salt and pepper
3 carrots, peeled and sliced
3 sticks celery, sliced
1 bouquet garni
Grated rind and juice of 1 large orange
600ml/1 pint good stock
15-25g/1/2-1oz cornflour
2 level tablespoons redcurrant jelly
4 tablespoons port or red wine
Hare's blood (if available)
Forcemeat balls (see opposite)
To garnish:
Parsley

BAKED HARE WITH CREAM SAUCE

JUGGED HARE

Place the wine, 2 tablespoons oil, marjoram, onion, bay leaves, cloves and seasonings in a bowl. Add the pieces of hare, cover and leave to marinate for at least 12 hours, turning several times. Remove the hare and dry. Fry the pieces of hare in the remaining oil until browned and transfer to a large casserole. Wipe out the pan, add the marinade, carrots, celery, bouquet garni, orange rind and juice, stock and seasonings to the pan and bring to the boil. Pour over the hare, cover the casserole tightly and cook in a moderate oven (160°C/ 325°F, Gas Mark 3) for 3-3 1/2 hours until very tender. Discard bay leaves and bouquet garni.

Strain off the cooking juices and thicken with cornflour blended in a little cold water. Add the redcurrant jelly and port and adjust the seasonings. Bring back to the boil, then, if liked, blend a little of the sauce with the hare's blood and return to the sauce. Do not allow to boil after adding the blood or it will curdle. Pour back over the hare. Serve with forcemeat balls and parsley.

Forcemeat balls:
75g/3oz fresh breadcrumbs
1 onion, peeled and finely chopped
1 apple, peeled, cored and grated
2 sticks celery, finely chopped
Grated rind of 1 lemon or orange
1 teaspoon lemon juice
Salt and pepper
1 egg, beaten

Combine all the ingredients and form into small balls. Place on a greased baking sheet and cook alongside the hare for the last 30-40 minutes of cooking time.

MINTED SADDLE OF HARE

The sauce is well flavoured with vinegar, wine, redcurrant jelly and freshly chopped mint.

1 saddle of hare
Salt and pepper
Few streaky bacon rashers,
(optional)
4 tablespoons oil
150ml/1/4 pint red wine
150ml/1/4 pint good stock
Grated rind of 1 lime or lemon
1 tablespoon wine vinegar
3 level tablespoons
redcurrant jelly
1-2 tablespoons lime or lemon juice
1/2 level teaspoon ground allspice
1-2 level tablespoons freshly
chopped mint
To garnish:
Fresh mint leaves
Lime or lemon wedges

Season the hare and if liked lay the bacon rashers over the joint. Stand in a roasting tin, cover with the oil and roast in a moderate oven (180°C/350°F, Gas Mark 4) for about 1-1 1/2 hours or until tender, basting several times. Remove from the tin and skim off the fat from the pan juices. Stir the wine, stock and fruit rind into the residue and then boil until beginning to become syrupy. Add the vinegar, jelly, lemon juice and allspice and simmer until dissolved and the sauce is smooth. Season to taste and add the mint, then simmer for a minute or so before serving the hare with a little sauce spooned over and the rest separately in a bowl.

Garnish with mint and lime or lemon wedges.
SERVES 4

**MINTED SADDLE
OF HARE**

Hare recipes

ANDALUSIAN HARE

Pieces of saddle of hare pot roasted on a bed of onion, pepper, olives and mushrooms and finished with yoghurt and fresh coriander.

Saddle of hare, cut into four portions
Little seasoned flour
2 tablespoons oil
2 cloves garlic, crushed
1 large onion, peeled and chopped
1 red pepper, deseeded and sliced
12 stuffed green olives, halved
12 black olives, stoned and halved
100g/4oz large mushrooms, thickly sliced
200ml/7fl oz stock
Salt and pepper
1/2 level teaspoon ground coriander
To garnish:
Natural yoghurt
Freshly chopped coriander or parsley

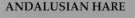

ANDALUSIAN HARE

SADDLE OF HARE
(pictured below)

Trim the hare and coat the pieces lightly in seasoned flour. Heat the oil in a pan and fry the pieces until well browned all over; remove from the pan and fry gently until soft then add the pepper and continue cooking for a few minutes. Add the olives and mushrooms and continue for a further 2-3 minutes. Add the stock and bring up to the boil. Season well with salt, pepper and coriander.

Transfer to a casserole and bury the pieces of hare in the vegetables. Cover tightly and cook in a cool oven (160°C/325°F, Gas Mark 3) for about 1 1/2 hours, until tender. Serve each portion on a bed of the vegetable mixture topped with a spoonful of yoghurt and sprinkled with freshly chopped coriander or parsley.
SERVES 4

SADDLE OF HARE

The saddle of the hare is pot-roasted after marinating.

1 saddle of hare
2 onions, peeled and sliced
2 carrots, peeled and sliced
2 cloves garlic, crushed
2 bay leaves
150ml/1/4 pint medium sherry
1-2 tablespoons brandy
8-10 rashers streaky bacon derinded
300ml/1/2 pint stock
300ml/1/2 pint single cream
40g/1 1/2oz butter or margarine
40g/1 1/2oz flour
Salt and pepper
100-175g/4-6oz green grapes, preferably seedless
2 tablespoons hare's blood (optional)
To garnish:
Watercress

Place the hare in a suitable container and surround with the onions, carrots, garlic and bay leaves. Pour the sherry and brandy over the hare, cover and leave to marinate for 12-24 hours, turning or basting occasionally.

Remove the saddle and drain well, then cover with the bacon rashers. Strain the marinade and put the vegetables in the base of a casserole and stand the saddle of hare on top. Pour the marinade back over the meat and vegetables and cover tightly. Cook in a moderate oven (180°C/350°F, Gas Mark 4) for $1^1/2$ hours, basting several times. Bring the stock to the boil, add the cream and boil until reduced by about one-third.

Cream the butter and flour together to make a beurre manie, and then gradually whisk into the cream sauce and bring up to the boil until thickened; adjust the seasonings.

Remove the hare to a serving dish and keep warm. Strain the cooking juices into the sauce and add most of the grapes. Simmer for 2 minutes. If using the hare's blood, blend this with a little of the sauce, mix well and return to the sauce, but do not allow to boil again or it will curdle. Serve the hare with some of the sauce spooned over and the remainder in a jug. Garnish with the remaining grapes and watercress.
SERVES 4-6

GOUJONS OF HARE WITH TARTARE SAUCE

An unusual way of serving hare, but the crispy coating adds a good texture.

1 young hare, jointed
Little oil
1 onion, peeled and sliced
Few whole cloves
450ml/³/4 pint stock
150ml/¹/4 pint red wine
Salt and pepper
1 egg, beaten
Golden breadcrumbs
Deep fat for frying
Tartare Sauce:
150ml/¹/4 pint thick mayonnaise
(or half mayonnaise half fromage
frais or yoghurt)
1 tablespoon lemon juice
8 gherkins, finely chopped
1 clove garlic, crushed
6-8 stuffed olives, chopped
1-2 tablespoons capers, chopped
2 level tablespoons freshly
chopped parsley
To garnish:
Lemon wedges and parsley sprigs

Brown the hare joints lightly in oil and place in a casserole. Fry the onion until soft and add to the casserole with the cloves, stock, wine and seasonings.

Cover and cook in a moderate oven (180°C/350°F, Gas Mark 4) for about $1^1/2$ hours or until almost tender. Leave until cold.

Strip the meat off the bones and cut into 2.5-4cm/1-1¹/2 in strips.

Dip the pieces of hare first in beaten egg, then coat in breadcrumbs. Chill until required. Heat the oil until a cube of bread will brown in 30 seconds. Fry the pieces of hare, a few at a time, until golden brown. Drain on absorbent paper and keep warm.

For the tartare sauce, mix all the ingredients together adding seasonings to taste. Serve the crispy goujons of hare garnished with lemon wedges and parsley, with the sauce in a separate bowl.
SERVES 4-6

Hare recipes

LEMON HARE WITH GARLIC

The marinade consists only of lemon, herbs and oil to keep the flesh moist and give flavour to the hare. The amount of garlic sounds overpowering but is not so!

1 hare, prepared and jointed
125ml/4fl oz lemon juice
6 tablespoons oil (vegetable or olive)
2 level tablespoons freshly chopped mixed herbs
300ml/^{1}/2 pint stock
250ml/8fl oz dry white wine
8-10 small cloves garlic, peeled
Salt and pepper
25g/1oz butter or margarine
25g/1oz flour
Hare's blood (if possible)
To garnish:
Parsley

Put the pieces of hare into a shallow container. Combine the lemon juice, 4 tablespoons of the oil and the herbs, and pour over the hare. Cover and marinate for 24 hours, in a cool place, turning several times. Remove the hare and drain well. Heat the remaining oil in a pan and fry the pieces of hare until well browned all over.

Add the marinade, herbs, stock, wine, garlic and seasonings and bring up to the boil. Cover and simmer gently for 3 hours.

Cream the butter and flour together to make a beurre manie and then gradually whisk into the sauce in small pieces. If the sauce is too thick, add a little more stock. Bring back to the boil and, if using the hare's blood, remove a little sauce and blend with the blood before returning to the pan;

do not allow to boil after adding the blood or the sauce will curdle. Adjust the seasonings and serve garnished with parsley.
SERVES 6

HARE PIE

A richly flavoured pie using hare and beef which need to marinate overnight to really bring out the flavour fully.

Marinade:
1 onion, peeled and finely chopped
1 stick celery, chopped
^{1}/2 level teaspoon ground coriander
8 juniper berries, crushed
2 bay leaves (fresh if possible)
1 level teaspoon dried marjoram
1 level tablespoon freshly chopped parsley or coriander
300ml/^{1}/2 pint red wine
3 tablespoons oil
Filling:
4 hare legs or ^{1}/2 hare
450g/1lb braising steak
175g/6oz pieces lean streaky bacon, derinded and chopped
2 tablespoons oil
175g/6oz button mushrooms
Salt and pepper
350g/^{3}/4lb puff pastry
Beaten egg or milk to glaze

Mix together all the ingredients for the marinade. Cut the hare flesh from the bones and dice; add to the marinade with the beef cut into 2.5cm/1in cubes. Cover and leave to marinate for 12-24 hours, turning once or twice.

For the filling, heat the bacon in a pan until the fat begins to run, then add the oil and mushrooms and cook

LEMON HARE WITH GARLIC

HARE PIE

gently for 2-3 minutes. Gradually stir in the marinade from the meat and bring up to the boil. Season well, add the hare and beef, cover and simmer very gently for about $1^1/2$ hours or until tender. Stir occasionally and add a little more wine or stock if becoming too dry. Adjust seasonings, turn into a pie dish with a funnel in the centre and leave to cool.

Roll out the pastry and cut a strip 2.5cm/1in wide; place on the dampened rim of the dish. Brush this strip with water and position the lid. Trim, flake and decorate the edges, make a hole in the centre and decorate with leaves cut from the pastry trimmings.

Glaze with beaten egg or milk and cook in a hot oven (220°C/425°F, Gas Mark 7) for 25-30 minutes.

Reduce oven temperature to moderately hot (190°C/375°F, Gas Mark 5) and continue for 15-25 minutes, covering with a sheet of greaseproof paper when sufficiently browned. Serve hot.
SERVES 6-8

FRUITED HARE WITH PRUNES AND APRICOTS

The flavouring with this method of jugging hare is very different but the sweetness of the fruit balances the richness of the hare very well and makes a delicious dinner party dish.

l hare, prepared and jointed
1 level teaspoon mixed spice
$1/2$ level teaspoon ground ginger
Salt and pepper
2 onions, peeled and sliced
2 bay leaves
450ml/$3/4$ pint brown ale
1 pint stock
75g/3oz no-need-to-soak prunes, stoned
75g/3oz no-need-to-soak dried apricots, halved
3 tablespoons wine vinegar
1 level tablespoon brown sugar
40g/$1^1/2$oz butter or margarine
40g/$1^1/2$oz flour
To garnish:
Chopped parsley

Wipe the hare all over and reserve any blood, if available. Combine the spices with the seasonings and rub all over the pieces of hare and place in a heavy ovenproof casserole.

Add the onions, bay leaves and brown ale, cover and leave to marinate for 24 hours in a cool place, turning at least once. Bring the stock to the boil, add to the casserole, cover and cook in a moderate oven (180°C/350°F, Gas Mark 4) for an hour.

Add the prunes and apricots, vinegar and sugar, mix well and return to the oven for another hour or until tender. Strain off the juices into a saucepan and boil hard until reduced to about 600ml/1 pint.

Meanwhile cream the fat and flour together to make a beurre manie then gradually whisk small knobs of it into the sauce bringing back to the boil until sufficiently thickened.

If using the hare's blood, add at the last minute and do not boil again. Adjust the seasonings and pour back over the hare. Serve each portion liberally sprinkled with chopped parsley.
SERVES 6-8

Note: suitable to freeze for up to 2 months, but without the addition of the blood.

SALMON
KING OF FRESHWATER FISH

THE SALMON is the king of freshwater fish. Caught by river anglers from February to August, salmon also spend much of their lives at sea where many are netted.

This very round fish generally weighs from a few pounds to 13 1/2kg/30lb. Young salmon are called grilse and make excellent eating. The salmon is an oily fish full of vitamin D with plenty of animal protein and some calcium. It has a higher calorific value and though rather less digestible than white fish, it has a wonderful, delicate flavour.

Salmon at its best should have a smallish head and tail with a thick neck. It should be stiff, red in the gills and with bright silvery scales. The raw flesh should be bright red; pink flesh indicates an inferior fish.Traditionally, salmon are poached and this is excellent provided you have a suitable cooking vessel. Fish kettles nowadays tend to be smaller than the old-fashioned types and are usually very expensive to buy, but if you are lucky enough to own one or can borrow one the problem should be solved.

However, the fish may be too large to fit in even a fish kettle. This can only be remedied by cutting the fish in half (or smaller) wrapping in foil and cooking the pieces separately. Once cooked the pieces can be skinned (boned if liked) and reassembled with suitable garnishes to cover the joins.

Another method of poaching is to use a large saucepan or preserving pan. Place a plate in the base and lower in the fish, supported by strips of treble-thickness foil (for easy removal), curving the fish to the shape of the pan. Not only does this solve the problem of finding a suitable container but it also gives an attractive shape and appearance to the cooked fish and even more scope for decoration.The other main method of cooking a whole salmon is to wrap it completely in well-buttered foil and bake in a cool oven (150°C/300°F, Gas Mark 2). Again the fish will need to be curved (unless very small) to fit into your oven, but the result is excellent.

Pieces of salmon and steaks may be poached, baked, cooked in foil, grilled, fried and barbecued and cooked in the microwave oven. Salmon will freeze very satisfactorily either whole, in sides, pieces or steaks and as fresh or smoked salmon. Cooked salmon dishes can also be frozen and it doesn't matter if the salmon has been frozen prior to cooking; once cooked it will freeze satisfactorily for up to two months. Raw salmon can be stored in the freezer for up to a year if the fish is large; cuts and steaks, on the other hand, are best if only stored for up to six months.

It is essential to thaw all raw salmon completely before cooking.

SALMON IN ASPIC
(pictured opposite, recipe on page 114)

GRAVAD LAX
(pictured below, recipe on page 108)

Salmon recipes

GRAVAD LAX

This Scandinavian dish is a delicious alternative to smoked salmon. It needs at least two, and preferably five, days of marinating and is traditionally served with a strong dill sauce.

900g/2lb tail-piece of fresh salmon (or larger if preferred)
1½ level tablespoons coarse sea salt
1½ level teaspoons coarsely ground black peppercorns
1½ level tablespoons granulated or demerara sugar
4 level tablespoons freshly chopped dill or 1½ level tablespoons dried dillweed
2 tablespoons brandy

Carefully bone the fish but leave the skin on. Make sure all the bones are removed with the help of a pair of tweezers. Wipe and dry the fish thoroughly. Mix together the salt, pepper, sugar, dill and brandy. Spread one-third of the pickling mixture on the bottom of a flat dish. Lay a piece of salmon, skin-side downwards on it and spread the cut surface with half the remaining pickle. Cover with the other piece of salmon with the skin upwards and spread with the rest of the pickle. Cover the dish with several layers of clingfilm and press down evenly with weights or a heavy object. Store in the refrigerator, turning the fish daily so it becomes evenly pickled.

To serve, scrape off the pickle and carve in very thin slices as for smoked salmon. As a starter all you need is brown bread and butter; or for a main meal offer new potatoes and a simple green salad. Gravad lax will keep in the refrigerator for 4-5 days.
SERVES ABOUT 10 (as a starter)

SALMON EN CROUTE

This dish is equally good served hot or cold with Hollandaise sauce. It takes a little time to prepare but is well worth the effort.

1.3-1.8kg/3-4lb salmon or sea-trout, gutted
Juice of 1 lemon
Salt and pepper
50g/2oz softened butter
2 level teaspoons freshly chopped dill or 1 level teaspoon dried dillweed
450g/1lb puff pastry
Beaten egg to glaze
Hollandaise sauce (see opposite)
To garnish:
Lettuce leaves
Lemon wedges
Cherry tomatoes

To fillet the fish, slip a sharp knife along the top of the backbone from tail to head keeping close to the backbone, and lift off the fillet. Turn the fish over and repeat with the second fillet. Remove the skin from the fish, again working from tail to head, lay the fish skin-side downwards and using a very sharp knife and a sawing action, gradually work along the length of the fish, pressing the knife firmly down onto the skin as you go. Remove any visible bones from the flesh with tweezers, if necessary. The head of the fish may be discarded or kept to help with the shape of the fish in pastry. Rub the flesh of the fish with lemon juice and season lightly. Lay one fillet on a flat surface spread with the softened butter and sprinkle with dill. Cover with the second fillet to reshape the fish. Roll out about 3/4 of the pastry fairly thinly. Stand the fish on the pastry with the head in place, if used; damp the edges and carefully enclose in the pastry keeping to the shape as much as possible and with the pastry joins underneath.

Transfer to a greased baking sheet, bending fish if necessary to fit. Roll out the remaining pastry. Glaze the whole fish with beaten egg. Cut fluted circles approx 7cm/2 1/2 inches in diameter and cut each in half. Lay these in overlapping rows to represent scales working from tail to head. Make a slightly enlarged tail from pastry, and an eye, position and then glaze overall again.

Cook in a hot oven (220°C/425°F, Gas Mark 7) for 30 minutes, then reduce temperature to moderately hot (190°C/375°C, Gas Mark 5) and continue for 20-30 minutes until golden brown. Lay a sheet of greaseproof paper over the pastry when sufficiently browned.

Garnish and serve hot with vegetables or cold with salad. Serve Hollandaise sauce separately in a bowl.
SERVES 6-10

Hollandaise Sauce:
6 tablespoons white wine vinegar
3 tablespoons water
10 black peppercorns
6 egg yolks
175-275g/6-10oz softened butter
Salt and white pepper
Lemon juice to taste

Put the vinegar, water and peppercorns into a pan and boil hard until reduced by almost half. Strain into the top of a double saucepan or heatproof bowl over a saucepan of simmering water and whisk in the egg yolks. Cook over very gently simmering water, stirring continuously, until thick but take care it does not 'scramble'. Beat in the butter a knob at a time until smooth, then season to taste with salt, pepper and lemon juice.

Cover and keep warm to serve with the salmon. The sauce may also be served cold if more convenient.

SALMON STEAKS WITH PORT WINE SAUCE

Port and salmon sounds a strange combination but, it makes a change to the more usual type of sauce.

4 fresh salmon steaks
100ml/4 fl oz port
100g/4oz butter
1-2 tablespoons mushroom ketchup
2-4 anchovy fillets, finely chopped
Salt and pepper
To garnish:
Watercress

Place the salmon steaks in a well-greased shallow ovenproof dish. Bring the port up to the boil in a small pan, then add butter in knobs, heating gently until melted, then add the ketchup, anchovies and seasoning to taste. Pour over the salmon, cover with a lid or foil and cook in a moderate oven (180°C/350°F, Gas Mark 4) for about 20 minutes or until the salmon is tender. Serve hot, garnished with watercress.

Alternatively, cook the salmon for only 15 minutes, then leave in the covered dish until cold and serve cold with new potatoes and salads.
SERVES 4

HOLLANDAISE SAUCE

SALMON STEAKS WITH PORT WINE SAUCE

Salmon recipes

SALMON AND COURGETTE QUICHE

An excellent way of using up the last trimmings from a whole salmon.

1 large courgette, trimmed and coarsely grated
150g/6oz shortcrust pastry (made using 150g/6oz plain flour etc)
1 level tablespoon freshly chopped tarragon or 1^1/2 level teaspoons dried tarragon
2-3 spring onions, chopped or 1 level tablespoon finely chopped onion
150-225g/6-8oz cooked salmon, flaked

2 eggs (size 2 or 3), beaten
150ml/^{1}/4 pint single cream or natural yoghurt
150ml/^{1}/4 pint milk
Salt and pepper
Pinch of ground nutmeg or allspice
50g/2oz mature Cheddar cheese, grated (optional)
To garnish:
Fresh tarragon
Mixed salads

Put the courgettes into a heatproof bowl and pour boiling water over; leave to stand for at least 10 minutes. Heat the oven to hot (220°C/425°F, Gas Mark 7) and put a baking sheet in to heat. Make up the pastry and use to line a 20cm/8in flan tin, dish or ring. Drain the courgettes very thoroughly, squeezing out all the excess water then mix with the tarragon, onion and salmon and put into the pastry case.

Beat together the eggs, cream, milk, seasonings and spice and pour over the salmon. If liked, sprinkle with the cheese.

Cook in the hot oven standing the quiche on the hot baking sheet for 20 minutes. Reduce the temperature to moderately hot (190°C/375°F, Gas Mark 5) and continue to cook for 20-25 minutes or until set and golden brown. Serve hot or cold garnished with fresh tarragon (if available) and mixed salads.
SERVES 4-6

Individual quiches –
Roll out the pastry and use to line four individual flan tins approx 11cm/4^1/2in or Yorkshire pudding tins and cook as above but reduce lower temperature cooking by about 10 minutes.

SALMON AND COURGETTE QUICHE
(pictured below)

SALMON AND SPINACH SOUFFLÉ

A hot soufflé which must be eaten straight from the oven. The salmon and spinach complement each other particularly well in this dish which makes an ideal summer supper.

175g/6oz cooked salmon, flaked
225g/8oz spinach, well chopped
150 ml/¼ pint natural yoghurt,
single cream or fromage frais
Salt and pepper
Ground coriander
3 eggs
25g/1oz butter or margarine
25g/1oz flour
150ml/¼ pint milk
50g/2 oz Cheddar cheese, grated
(optional)

Mix the salmon with two-thirds of the spinach and the yoghurt, cream or fromage frais, and season with salt, pepper and coriander to taste. Put into the base of a well-greased soufflé dish or ovenproof dish (approx 19 cm/ ¹/2in). Separate the eggs. Melt the butter in a pan, stir in the flour and cook for a minute or so.

Gradually stir in the milk and bring to the boil, stirring all the time to give a very thick sauce.

Cool slightly then beat in the cheese, remaining spinach and plenty of seasonings and then beat in the egg yolks one at a time. Whisk the egg whites until very stiff and fold evenly through the sauce.

Pour into the prepared dish over the salmon and bake at once in a fairly hot oven (200°C/400°F, Gas Mark 6) for about 35 minutes or until well risen and browned.

Serve immediately before it sinks!
SERVES 4

BAKED SALMON

The alternative method to poaching salmon is baking. The fish, if large, can be curved before wrapping in foil, which allows quite a large fish to fit into the oven.

1.25-1.5 kg/3-3¹/2lb salmon or
sea-trout, cleaned
Salt and pepper
2-3 fresh bay leaves
Butter
Hollandaise sauce (see page 109)
To garnish:
Cucumber
Mustard and cress
Lemon wedges
Cherry tomatoes
Salads

Season the fish lightly inside with salt and pepper and place the bay leaves evenly along the inside of the fish. Put onto a large piece of well-buttered foil, curving the fish if necessary to fit into the oven. Package the fish loosely and stand on a baking sheet or in a roasting tin. Cook in a cool oven (150°C/300°F, Gas Mark 2) for 1-1¹/4 hours. Leave in the foil for 15 minutes then unwrap carefully, remove the skin from the fish and place on a hot serving dish.

Garnish with slices of cucumber, mustard and cress and with lemon wedges and cherry tomatoes and serve with new potatoes and Hollandaise sauce.

If the fish is to be served cold, then leave wrapped in the foil until quite cold before removing the skin and chilling thoroughly. It may be glazed with aspic and decorated as for the poached fish.
SERVES 6-10

Salmon recipes

SALMON MOUSSE

A mousse of salmon looks very impressive if served in a fish-shaped mould, but it will, of course, taste just as good if set in a plain bowl or individual dishes. Decorate the mousse with slices of cucumber and stuffed olives and top with a layer of aspic for a really professional finish.

275-350g/10-12oz cooked salmon, flaked
25g/1oz butter or margarine
25g/1oz flour
300ml/^{1}/$_2$ pint milk
^{1}/$_4$ level teaspoon dry mustard
Good pinch of cayenne pepper
Salt and pepper
2 tablespoons wine vinegar
2 eggs (size 1 or 2), separated
150ml/^{1}/$_4$ pint double cream
4 level teaspoons powdered gelatine
To garnish:
Stuffed or black olives
Whole prawns
Cucumber
Liquid aspic jelly

Melt the butter in a pan, stir in the flour and cook for one minute. Gradually add the milk and bring up to the boil. Add the mustard, cayenne, salt and pepper to taste, and the vinegar and simmer for 2 minutes. Beat in the egg yolks and simmer for a further minute stirring continuously. Remove from the heat and stir in flaked salmon. Lightly whip the cream until thick but not stiff and fold through the sauce.

Dissolve the gelatine in 3 tablespoons water in a small basin over a pan of hot water, or in a microwave set to cool. Cool slightly then stir evenly into the salmon mixture. Leave until on the point of setting and then fold in the stiffly beaten egg whites. Pour into an oiled fish mould, a serving dish or individual dishes and chill until quite set.

To serve, turn the fish out of the mould carefully, after easing the sides away from the mould, onto a dish or board. Garnish with olives, whole prawns and slices of cucumber together with chopped set aspic jelly if liked. If in dishes, decorate the tops with slices of olive and cucumber, top with aspic and when set add whole prawns to complete.
SERVES 8

Note: Can be frozen without the jellied topping for up to 2 months.

POTTED SALMON

A tasty way of serving salmon using steaks. Although they are best flaked and covered with butter, the steaks can be served cold, as they are, with a good home-made mayonnaise.

6 salmon steaks (approx 175g/6oz each)
^{1}/$_2$ level teaspoon each of ground nutmeg, ground mace, ground cloves and white pepper
100g/4oz butter
100g/4oz finely chopped or minced raw onion
4 fresh bay leaves
4-6 anchovy fillets
75g/3oz clarified butter (see below)

Wipe the salmon steaks and trim if necessary. Combine the spices and use to season the steaks thoroughly. Arrange in an ovenproof dish in layers with flakes of butter between. Sprinkle with the onion and lay the bay leaves and anchovy fillets on top. Dot with the remaining butter, cover with foil and cook in a moderate oven (180°C/350°F, Gas Mark 4) for 30-40 minutes. Remove the salmon, drain and then discard the skin and bones. Flake or pound the salmon flesh and pack tightly into one dish or into 6 individual dishes. Moisten with a little of the cooking juices and leave to cool.

Cover with a layer of clarified butter and chill before serving.
SERVES 6

Clarified Butter:
Melt the butter very gently in a pan or bowl in a warm oven. The sediment will sink to the bottom and the clear butter should be poured or spooned off carefully ready for use.

Note: The salmon may also be puréed in a food processor, adding sufficient of the cooking juices to barely moisten, and then be packed into dishes.

SALMON PARCELS

Filo pastry is good for keeping in the juices and flavour of the fish and gives a splendid crispy outer layer.

4 fresh salmon steaks or pieces of fillet of salmon, skinned and boned
2 tablespoons dry white wine
2 tablespoons raspberry or blackcurrant vinegar (or red wine vinegar)
2 level teaspoons crushed coriander seeds or 3/4 level teaspoon ground coriander
1 level tablespoon freshly chopped fennel or dill
Salt and pepper
75g/3oz butter
100g/4oz button mushrooms, sliced
6 sheets filo pastry
2 level teaspoons arrowroot
2 tablespoons double cream
To garnish:
Sprigs of fennel, dill or parsley

Put the pieces of salmon into a small dish in a single layer. Combine the wine, vinegar, coriander, fennel or dill and a little freshly ground black pepper and pour over the salmon. Mix well, cover and leave for an hour or so. Melt 25g/1oz butter and fry the mushrooms lightly, drain and reserve the liquor. Melt the remaining butter. Cut each sheet of filo pastry in half to give 12 squares. Brush each sheet of pastry with butter and layer three sheets together to give four separate piles of pastry.

Place one well-drained piece of salmon on each piece of filo and divide the mushrooms between them placing on the fish. Either fold up completely to give neat parcels or gather the corners together and squeeze firmly to give 'bundles'. Place on a greased baking sheet and brush again all over with melted butter. Cook in a fairly hot oven (220°C/400°F, Gas Mark 6) for 15 minutes or until the pastry is lightly browned and crisp. Mix the marinade with the mushroom liquor and arrowroot in a small pan and bring slowly to the boil, stirring continuously. Stir in the cream and reheat gently. If too thick add a touch of milk or water, then adjust the seasonings and serve with the parcels, garnished with fennel, dill or parsley.
SERVES 4

SALMON PARCELS

Salmon recipes

SALMON IN ASPIC
(pictured on page 106)

One of the traditional methods of serving cold salmon. It makes a most attractive centre piece to a buffet table and can be cooked either flat or curved for effect.

1.8-2.7 kg/4-6 lb fresh salmon, cleaned with head left on
300 ml/^{1}/2 pint white wine vinegar
1 onion, peeled and thinly sliced
1 carrot, peeled and sliced
1 lemon, thinly sliced
3-4 bay leaves
1 level teaspoon whole black peppercorns
To decorate:
Cucumber slices and skin
Stuffed olives
Lemon
Salads
Cherry tomatoes
Aspic jelly (approx 450ml/^{3}/4 pint)

Wipe the fish inside and out and if liked put the bay leaves inside the fish. Half fill a fish kettle or preserving pan with water. Add the wine vinegar, onion, carrot, lemon, bay leaves (if not inside the fish) and peppercorns and bring up to the boil.

Carefully lower in the salmon, curving it if using a preserving pan and using strips of foil to help lift it into the water evenly.

Return to the boil and then simmer very gently – the water *must not* boil, only simmer – allowing about 8 minutes to each 450g/1 lb. Leave the fish in the water in a cool place until cold then carefully remove from the water and strip off the skin. Chill the fish.

Make up the aspic jelly following the directions on the packet and, when cold, chill half of it. When this aspic begins to thicken brush a layer over the whole fish, including the head. Repeat two or three times to give an even coating and chilling between each application.

Next decorate the fish using slices of cucumber, thin strips of cucumber skin, slices of stuffed olive etc, dipping in the aspic so it will stick to the fish. Finally give another one or two coats of aspic, using the reserved jelly as that, too, thickens.

Leave any excess aspic to set and then chop to use as decoration around the fish together with salad, lemon slices or wedges and cherry tomatoes. SERVES 8-16

SALMON COCOTTES

This makes a very special breakfast or brunch dish, or is equally appetising as either a starter or a light lunch.

Approx 150g/6 oz smoked salmon or cooked flaked fresh salmon
4 large eggs
Salt and black pepper
Squeeze of lemon juice
Pinch of dried dillweed (optional)
4-6 tablespoons double or single cream
40g/1^{1}/2oz Edam or Gouda cheese (optional)
To garnish:
Parsley

Line four small ramekin dishes with smoked salmon so it fits neatly or divide the flaked salmon between the dishes. Break an egg carefully into each dish and season lightly with salt and pepper, and add a squeeze of lemon juice to each and a small pinch of dillweed, if liked. Spoon the cream carefully over the eggs and sprinkle with cheese if you are using it.

Stand on a baking sheet for a crispy baked finish or put into a tin containing about 2.5 cm/1in water and cover with foil for a more poached finish. Cook either way in a moderate oven (180°C/350°F, Gas Mark 4) for 12-14 minutes until just set.

Garnish with sprigs of parsley and serve with hot fingers of toast.
SERVES 4

PICKLED SALMON

Another way of serving salmon which is only barely cooked and then marinated in wine vinegar and herbs for a few days before eating.

Ideal for a starter or a main course dish, and the remains make delicious sandwiches.

900g/2lb fresh salmon, filleted
1 small onion, peeled and sliced
2 carrots, peeled and sliced
1 large sprig each of fresh parsley,
thyme and tarragon (or $^1/4$ level
teaspoon of each herb, dried)
1 level teaspoon black
peppercorns
300ml/$^1/2$ pint white wine
vinegar
Salt and pepper

After filleting the salmon put it back together again and tie in place with cotton, if necessary. Place in a saucepan and barely cover with water. Bring to the boil and simmer gently for 12-15 minutes. Remove the salmon at once, drain and leave until cold.

Add the onion, carrots herbs, vinegar and seasonings to the fish

stock, bring to the boil and simmer for 15 minutes until slightly reduced. Remove the cotton and skin from the fish and place in a deep dish.

Pour the hot marinade over it and cover. When cold, refrigerate and turn the salmon over carefully in the marinade, night and morning for 2-3 days. Drain the fish and serve with salads.
SERVES 6

PICKLED SALMON
(pictured below)

Salmon recipes

SALMON ST JACQUES

This recipe can be served on a bed of rice, in individual dishes with piped creamed potatoes or mixed with pasta.

450 g/1 lb fresh salmon
4 tablespoons dry white wine
1 bay leaf
salt and pepper
40g/1½ oz butter or margarine
25g/1 oz flour
100g/4 oz button mushrooms
Pinch of ground allspice
2-3 tablespoons double cream
675-900 g/1½-2lb creamed potatoes
Few dried breadcrumbs
 To garnish:
Parsley and lemon

Put the salmon into a small saucepan with the wine, bay leaf, seasonings and a little water to barely cover it. Bring to the boil, cover and poach gently for about 10 minutes until cooked through. Drain and leave to cool a little, then skin, discard bones and flake roughly. Melt the butter in a pan and fry the quartered mushrooms gently for 1-2 minutes. Stir in the flour and cook for a minute or so. Gradually work in about 200ml/⅓ pint cooking liquor and bring up to the boil.

Simmer for a minute until thickened then stir in a pinch of allspice, salt and pepper to taste, the cream and the flaked salmon. Pipe the potato around the outside of four small ovenproof dishes or scallop shells and lightly brown under the grill or in a hot oven (220°C/425°F, Gas Mark 7). Spoon in the hot salmon mixture, sprinkle with a few dried breadcrumbs and just lightly brown under the grill or in the oven. Garnish with lemon and parsley.
SERVES 4

SALMON KEDGEREE

An old favourite with a new twist.

275g/10 oz long grain rice
Salt and pepper
225g/8oz cooked salmon, flaked
1 large onion, peeled and chopped
50g/2oz butter
100g/4oz button mushrooms sliced
Little ground coriander
2 level tablespoons freshly
chopped parsley
2 hard-boiled eggs, chopped
6-8 tablespoons single cream

Cook the rice in plenty of boiling salted water until just tender, drain, rinse under hot water and drain very thoroughly again. Make sure all bones and skin are discarded from the fish. Fry the onion very gently in the melted butter until soft, but only lightly coloured. Add the mushrooms and continue for a few minutes more. Season well with salt, pepper and coriander then add the salmon and heat through thoroughly. Add the rice, parsley and chopped eggs and heat through again. Just before serving add the cream. Serve very hot.
SERVES 4

Note: Can be frozen for up to 2 months, but do not add the hard-boiled eggs until just before serving.

MICROWAVE SALMON STEAKS
Fish cooks beautifully in the microwave oven. Keep warm while making the sauce and serve at once.

4 salmon steaks (2.5 cm/1in thick)
4 tablespoons water
1 tablespoon lemon juice
Salt and pepper

SALMON ST JACQUES

SALMON KEDGEREE

MICROWAVE
SALMON STEAKS

Sauce:
2 egg yolks
4 tablespoons double cream
1 level tablespoon freshly chopped dill or parsley
To garnish:
Fresh herbs and lemon

Put the salmon in a shallow microwave-proof dish in a single layer. Mix the water and lemon juice together and pour over the fish. Season lightly. Cover with clingfilm and make two slits in the top. Cook on maximum (100%) for 6 minutes.

For the sauce, beat the egg yolks and cream together then strain in the fish cooking liquor. About $1/2$ level teaspoon cornflour may be blended in as well to act as a stabiliser. Put into a basin and cook on maximum (100%) for $2^1/2$ minutes, stirring every 30 seconds. Stir in seasonings to taste, add the herbs and serve garnished with herbs and lemon on a bed of the sauce or with sauce spooned over.
SERVES 4

SALMON AND AVOCADO RICE

One of the many ways of serving left-over cooked salmon.

225g/8oz cooked fresh salmon, roughly flaked
175g/6oz long grain rice
Salt and pepper
1 can anchovy fillets in oil
3 tablespoons milk
6-8 tablespoons French dressing (see right)
6 spring onions, trimmed and sliced or 2 level tablespoons finely chopped onion
2 level tablespoons freshly chopped parsley

8 black olives, halved and stoned
1 ripe avocado
Juice of 1 lemon
Lettuce leaves
To garnish:
Whole black olives

Cook the rice in plenty of boiling, salted water until tender, about 14 minutes, then drain, rinse under running water and drain thoroughly. Turn into a bowl and leave until cold. Drain the anchovies, dry on absorbent kitchen paper, then soak in the milk for 20 minutes or so to remove excess saltiness. Drain and cut in half lengthwise and then into lengths of approx 4cm/$1^1/2$ in. Mix the dressing, onions, parsley, anchovies and olives together, then add the flaked salmon.

Dice half the avocado, toss in lemon juice and add to the salad. Season and add to the rice and toss together. Turn into a serving dish lined with lettuce leaves and garnish with the remaining avocado, peeled sliced and dipped in lemon juice, and with black olives.
SERVES 4

French Dressing:
200ml/7 fl oz oil (salad, vegetable, olive or nut)
2-3 tablespoons white wine vinegar
1 tablespoon lemon juice
1 level teaspoon caster sugar
1 level teaspoon dry mustard
$1/2$ level teaspoon French mustard
1 clove garlic, crushed
Salt and freshly ground black pepper

Put all the ingredients into a screw-topped jar and shake very vigorously until completely emulsified. Store in a cool place and shake well before use.

SALMON AND AVOCADO RICE

TROUT
A DELICATE FLAVOUR

THERE ARE three types of trout. Rainbow trout is probably the best known because of its wider availability in shops and colourful body. The brown trout, too, is an excellent fish which lives in the rivers and mountain streams and is generally brownish with speckles. All trout have a delicately flavoured flesh requiring very little enhancement.

The largest of the trout is the sea-trout, sometimes called sewin or, less correctly, salmon-trout. It is much smaller than the true salmon, having a pale pink flesh, but is quite delicious and preferred by many for its delicate flavour and texture, to true salmon. The brown trout also can be quite large and this will feed several people rather than the usually individually sized rainbow trout.

The trout farms which have sprung up everywhere and enable all to go and 'choose their fish' concentrate mainly on the rainbow variety but some prefer to stock the brown trout. They are fed on a mixture containing shrimps which gives a pink tinge to the flesh.

Occasionally trout will have a muddy-flavoured flesh. Unfortunately this is due to the fish eating from the muddy beds of the rivers and streams and there is very little which can be done to help. It is quite safe to eat these fish but the taste is not very appetising. Large trout, especially sea-trout, may be cooked as for salmon by poaching, baking, grilling and the salmon recipes can also be made with trout. Smaller trout may be baked in the oven uncovered, covered or wrapped in foil; grilled, fried, poached and barbecued. And of course trout can be successfully smoked. They should be served skinned and with the head left on or removed but with the tail intact. They may be boned and reassembled or left on the bone. Fresh trout should be served with the heads and tails still on; unless you have a horror of heads. The eyes turn white when cooked and they may be left as they are or removed and replaced with a piece of stuffed olive or a small parsley sprig.

All types of trout will freeze well. It is best to gut them before freezing and use them as fresh as possible. They will keep in the freezer for up to 6 months. Thaw completely before use, but once thawed use immediately.

STUFFED TROUT
(pictured opposite, recipe on page 124)

FILLETS OF TROUT WITH SAFFRON
(pictured below, recipe on page 125)

Trout recipes

TROUT WITH MUSHROOMS

Poached trout served on a bed of mushrooms, cooked with wine and peppers.

This dish is equally delicious served cold.

4 trout, cleaned
4 large open mushrooms
550g/1¼lb cup mushrooms
100ml/4fl oz dry white
wine
Salt and pepper
2 onions, peeled
1 small green pepper,
deseeded and sliced
1 lemon

Put the fish and the four open mushrooms into a shallow, ovenproof dish. Pour over the wine and season with salt and pepper.

Cover and poach in a moderately hot oven (190°C/375°F, Gas Mark 5) for about 25 minutes.

Mince the cup mushroooms, the onions and half the green pepper.

Strain the wine from the fish into a shallow pan and add the mushroom, onion and pepper mixture.

Season well, add the juice of half the lemon and simmer gently, uncovered, until all the liquid has evaporated.

Remove the skin from the fish carefully, but leave the heads and tails on. Spoon the mushroom mixture onto a hot serving dish and arrange fish on top.

Put a 'collar' of green pepper on each fish and garnish with slices of lemon and the whole mushrooms.

Serve with boiled new potatoes and a green vegetable or salad.
SERVES 4

CRUNCHY TROUT

A mixture of oatmeal and chopped almonds are used to coat the fish before frying or baking and a butter and caper sauce is served with them.

4 trout, cleaned
4 level tablespoons medium
oatmeal
50g/2oz blanched almonds, finely
chopped
1 egg, beaten
40g/1½oz butter
2 tablespoons olive oil
Sauce:
50g/2oz butter
2 tablespoons capers
2 tablespoons lemon juice
Salt and pepper
To garnish:
Lemon wedges
Parsley sprigs

Wipe the trout inside and out. Combine the oatmeal and almonds. dip the trout first in the beaten egg and then coat in the almond mixture. Heat the butter and oil in a large frying pan and fry the trout gently for about 5 minutes each side, turning carefully so the coating does not fall off, until cooked through.

Alternatively place the fish in a well-greased ovenproof dish, head to tail and cook in a moderate oven (180°C/350°F, Gas Mark 4) for about 30 minutes or until cooked through and the coating is brown and crispy. Keep the fish warm.

For the sauce, melt the butter in a saucepan, add the capers and lemon juice, season to taste and heat through thoroughly. Serve with the fish garnished with lemon and parsley.
SERVES 4

TROUT WITH CREAMED CUCUMBER

A thick creamy sauce with pieces of cucumber added gives an attractive appearance and flavour to fresh trout.

4 trout, cleaned
4 level tablespoons seasoned flour
50g/2 oz butter
1-2 tablespoons dry white wine or stock
150ml/^{1}/4 pint double cream
Salt and pepper
^{1}/2 cucumber, cut into sticks or into balls with a melon baller
To garnish:
Lemon wedges and freshly chopped parsley

Toss the trout in the seasoned flour. Heat the butter in a large frying pan and fry the trout for about 5-6 minutes on each side until golden and just cooked through. Alternatively, cook under a moderate grill after liberally brushing with melted butter. Remove the trout from the pan and keep warm. Add the wine and cream to the pan, stir well and bring to the boil. Continue boiling rapidly to reduce the sauce to a thick, creamy consistency. Add the cucumber and heat through. Serve the trout with the sauce poured over the top and garnished with lemon wedges and chopped parsley.
SERVES 4

BROWN TROUT BAKED IN SALT

A different way to bake a whole large trout which encases the fish in salt and keeps all the juices in.

1-1.5kg/2-3lb brown trout, cleaned
Approx 1kg/2lb salt
Lemon slices

Garlic mayonnaise:
4-6 tablespoons thick mayonnaise
2 tablespoons double or soured cream
1-2 cloves garlic, crushed
2 level tablespoons freshly chopped parsley
Garlic dressing:
4 tablespoons oil
2 tablesoons lemon juice
Salt and pepper
2 cloves garlic, crushed
Finely grated rind of ^{1}/2 lemon
^{1}/2 level teaspoon caster sugar
2 level tablespoons freshly chopped herbs (optional)

Wipe the fish inside and out and place slices of lemon in the cavity. Brush lightly all over with oil or water. Put a layer of salt in an ovenproof dish just large enough to take the fish or in a foil lined roasting tin so it can be moulded to the shape of the fish.

Press the fish into the salt and cover with the remaining salt. Bake in a moderate oven (180°C/350°F, Gas Mark 4) for about 45 minutes, spooning the salt back over the fish after 15 minutes, as some will have slid off; it will then bake into a crust.

Meanwhile, combine the ingredients for the mayonnaise in one small bowl and combine the ingredients for the dressing in another, adding the herbs if liked.

To serve, break off the salt crust, taking the skin of the fish with it. Put the fish onto individual plates, garnish with lemon and serve with the two dressings.
SERVES 4-6

Note: The salt can be used several times for baking fish.

TROUT WITH CREAMED CUCUMBER

BROWN TROUT BAKED IN SALT

Trout recipes

TROUT WITH ALMONDS AND CUCUMBER

Oven-baked fish with an almond topping and sweet/sour cucumber.

4 trout, cleaned
4 slices lemon
Salt and pepper
40g/1¹/₂oz butter, melted
Sweet and sour cucumber:
¹/₂ cucumber
6 tablespoons white wine vinegar
2 tablespoons water
6 level tablespoons caster sugar
Freshly chopped parsley and/or fresh fennel

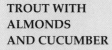

TROUT WITH ALMONDS AND CUCUMBER
(pictured below)

TROUT AND BACON PIE

Topping:
50g/2oz butter
50g/2oz flaked almonds
Juice of 1 lemon

Place a slice of lemon in the cavity of each trout and lay in a lightly greased shallow ovenproof dish. Season well and pour the butter overall. Cook in a moderately hot oven (190°C/375°F, Gas Mark 5) for 30-40 minutes or until just cooked through. Meanwhile, slice the cucumber evenly but not too thinly and place in a shallow dish. Put the vinegar and water in a pan and bring to the boil. Add the sugar and stir until dissolved, then simmer for a few minutes until slightly syrupy. Pour over the cucumber and leave to stand.

For the topping, melt the butter in a pan and fry the almonds gently until lightly browned. Remove from the heat and quickly add the lemon juice, stirring until they stop sizzling. Season to taste and reheat gently.

To serve, arrange the fish on a large dish and place the drained cucumber all around them. Spoon the almond mixture over the fish and sprinkle the cucumber with the herbs.
SERVES 4

TROUT AND BACON PIE

It is simple to fillet a fish and the fillets can be rolled up to put in a pie.

4 trout, filleted and skinned (see opposite)
175g/6oz streaky bacon rashers, derinded and chopped
1 onion, peeled and thinly sliced
2 eating apples
Salt and pepper
1 level tablespoon freshly chopped parsley

Good pinch of dried thyme
150ml/¼ pint single cream
Pastry:
225g/8oz plain flour
50g/2oz margarine
50g/2oz lard or white fat
Cold water to mix
1 level tablespoon sesame seeds
(optional)

Halve each fillet of fish and roll up roughly. Place in a fairly shallow pie dish. Fry the bacon in its own fat until the fat begins to run. Add the onion and cook gently until lightly browned. Drain and sprinkle over the fish. Peel, core and slice the apples and add to the dish. Season well and sprinkle with thyme and parsley. Remove a teaspoon of the cream for the glaze and pour the rest over the pie mixture.

For the pastry, sift the flour with a pinch of salt into a bowl and rub in the fats until the mixture resembles fine breadcrumbs. Add sufficient water to mix to a pliable dough. Roll out on a floured surface and cut off a strip approx 2.5cm/1in wide and place on the dampened rim of the dish. Brush this strip with water and position the lid. Press the edges well together, trim and crimp. Use the pastry trimmings to decorate the top, make a hole in the centre and glaze with the rest of the cream. Sprinkle with sesame seeds and cook in a fairly hot oven (200°C/400°F, Gas Mark 6) for about 45 minutes.
SERVES 4-5

Note: to fillet the fish, first cut off the head and then, using a sharp knife and beginning at the tail, strip the flesh off the bones, keeping the knife pressed firmly down onto the bones. Turn the fish over and repeat with the second side. Remove any loose bones.

To skin the fish, place skin-side down on a board (sprinkled with a little salt if it tends to slip) and, working from tail to head, strip the flesh from the skin keeping the knife at an angle to the skin and pressing firmly downwards as you work along.

TROUT WITH MUSTARD SAUCE

Grilled fish served with a piquant mustard sauce.

4 trout, cleaned
Salt and pepper
40g/1½oz butter or
margarine (melted)
40g/1½oz butter or margarine
1 small onion, peeled and finely
chopped
150ml/¼ pint single cream
2 level teaspoons French mustard
Good pinch dry mustard
2 teaspoons lemon juice
To garnish:
Lemon slices, chopped parsley
and gherkin fans

Wipe the fish all over and season lightly. Stand in a greased grill pan and brush all over with melted fat. Cook under a moderate grill for about 5 minutes each side, brushing again with melted fat when turning the fish. Remove and keep warm. Melt the rest of the fat in a pan and fry the onion gently until soft but not coloured. Add the cream, seasonings, mustards and lemon juice and heat gently for 2-3 minutes, without boiling. Adjust the seasonings and pour over the fish. Garnish with lemon slices dipped in chopped parsley and gherkin fans.
SERVES 4

**TROUT WITH
MUSTARD SAUCE**

Trout recipes

STUFFED TROUT

(pictured on page 118)

This recipe calls for boning the fish, filling with stuffing and rolling up before they are baked.

4 fresh trout, cleaned
4 heaped tablespoons fresh white breadcrumbs
1 level tablespoon freshly chopped parsley
Grated rind of ½ lemon
1 small onion, peeled and grated
1 clove garlic, crushed
2 hard-boiled eggs, chopped
25g/1oz shelled walnuts, chopped
Salt and pepper
2 tablespoons mayonnaise
To garnish:
Lemon wedges and parsley sprigs

Remove the heads from the fish and cut right along the stomachs to the tails. To remove the backbones place the fish flesh-side down on a board and press the thumb firmly along the backbone to loosen it. Turn the fish over and carefully ease the bone out and remove any other visible bones.

Combine the breadcrumbs, parsley, lemon rind, onion, garlic, chopped eggs, walnuts and plenty of seasonings and bind together with the mayonnaise. Spread the stuffing over the trout and roll up carefully from head to tail, securing with wooden cocktail sticks. Place in a lightly greased shallow ovenproof dish, cover with buttered foil and cook in a moderately hot oven (190°C/375°F, Gas Mark 5) for about 30 minutes or until cooked through. Remove the cocktail sticks and serve hot, garnished with lemon and parsley.
SERVES 4

BROWN TROUT WITH ORANGE SAUCE

Bake or poach the trout and serve it with a delicious creamy orange sauce.

1-1.5kg/2-3lb brown trout
Little softened butter
1 lemon, thinly sliced
3 egg yolks
3 tablespoons double cream
6 tablespoons dry white wine
1 tablespoon lemon juice
Grated rind of 1 small orange
Juice of 2 small oranges
Salt and pepper
Good pinch of cayenne pepper
50g/2oz butter, softened
To garnish:
Orange slices
Parsley or watercress

Wipe the trout all over and if baking lay on a well-greased sheet of foil and place the lemon slices in the cavity. Package loosely and stand in a roasting tin. Cook in a very moderate oven (160°C/325°F, Gas Mark 3) for 35-45 minutes. If poaching, place in a saucepan (curling it around if necessary to make it fit) and barely cover with water. Add the sliced lemon and a teaspoon of black peppercorns and 2 bay leaves. Bring up to the boil and simmer very gently for 20-30 minutes.

For the sauce, beat together the egg yolks, cream, wine, lemon juice, orange rind and juice in a heatproof bowl. Stand over a pan of gently simmering water and heat gently, stirring all the time, until the sauce is the consistency of thick pouring cream. Season to taste with salt, pepper and a pinch of cayenne then beat in the butter a little at a time.

Arrange the fish on a warmed serving dish, removing the skin if liked, and serve with orange slices and parsley or watercress, and with the warm sauce.
SERVES 4-6

FILLETS OF TROUT WITH SAFFRON *(pictured on page 119)*

Gently poached fillets of trout are served with a saffron and cream sauce.

4 large fresh trout, filleted
1 small onion, peeled and very finely chopped
25g/1oz butter or margarine
150ml/1/4 pint good fish stock
4-6 tablespoons dry vermouth or white wine
Salt and pepper
150ml/1/4 pint double or soured cream
Few strands saffron or 1/2 level teaspoon turmeric
1 level teaspoon freshly chopped dill or parsley
To garnish:
Sprigs of dill or parsley
Spring onion tassles

Fry the onion gently in the melted butter until soft but not coloured. Add the fish stock, vermouth or wine and seasonings and bring up to the boil. Add the fillets of trout, return to the boil, and simmer very gently for 4-5 minutes until just cooked. Drain and place on a serving dish; keep warm.

Boil the cooking juices until reduced by about one-third. Add the cream and saffron or turmeric and bring back to the boil for a minute or so. Stir in dill or parsley and adjust the seasonings. Pour over the fish and serve with dill or parsley and spring onions.
SERVES 4

POACHED TROUT WITH TARRAGON

Fresh trout are more often grilled or fried, but poaching is a very simple method and is especially good as it tends to keep the flesh of the fish really succulent. The tarragon adds a distinctive flavour.

4 fresh trout, cleaned
150ml/1/4 pint water
1 lemon
1 small onion, peeled and finely chopped
Salt and pepper
1 level tablespoon freshly chopped parsley
2 level tablespoons freshly chopped tarragon
or 1 level tablespoon dried tarragon
300ml/1/2 pint single cream

Keep the heads on the fish and arrange them head to tail in a large frying pan or flameproof casserole with a lid. Add the water, 2 thinly pared strips of lemon rind and the lemon juice, the onion and seasonings. Add half the parsley and half the tarragon and bring slowly to the boil. Cover the pan and simmer very gently for 15 minutes.

When cooked, carefully remove the fish to a serving dish, draining off all the excess liquid and keep warm. Boil the fish cooking liquor rapidly until reduced by half, then add the cream and reheat to just below boiling.

Season to taste and strain over the fish (or if preferred serve in a separate jug).

Sprinkle the fish with remaining herbs and serve at once.
SERVES 4

FILLETS OF TROUT WITH SAFFRON

POACHED TROUT WITH TARRAGON

GAME PIES AND COOKED GAME DISHES

A RAISED game pie makes a really spectacular centrepiece for a buffet table and this type of pie has been well-known since Elizabethan times, though the filling has changed somewhat since those days! Pies can be made with all types of pastry and served hot or cold. Sometimes raw ingredients are used to fill a hot-water crust pie, while in other recipes a mixture of raw and cooked ingredients is used, sometimes adding a layer of stuffing too. The meats may be finely or coarsely minced, chopped or cut into narrow strips.

Hot-water crust pastry is very malleable and can be used to line game pie moulds, cake tins or loaf tins or be raised by hand to whatever shape you require – given a little practice and with the help of something round which to mould the pastry. However, the pastry must be kept warm once made, by covering with a cloth while part of it is rolled out; if allowed to get cold it will become hard and brittle and useless for moulding or rolling.

Once cooked the pie is filled up with a well-flavoured stock containing gelatine which sets when the pie is chilled, leaving no empty spaces in the pie. Cooked raised pies will keep for several days, but are not good for freezing as the pastry becomes very brittle on thawing, making the slicing of the pie particularly difficult.

Other types of game pies are made using just a top crust which can be of short-crust, puff, flaky or suet-crust pastry and most can be served hot or cold. The fillings can be of one type of game or a mixture, or in some cases game mixed with beef. Use portions or pieces of game (a good way to use up legs and so on, where the breasts have been removed for another recipe) and pre-cook where necessary. Double crust pies can also be made using game, as can individual pasties.

Cooked game, whether specially cooked or left-over, lends itself well to made-up dishes, a great variety of which can be invented; or you can adapt many old favourites. If cooking the game specially, it is advisable to slightly undercook for it will continue to cook as the food cools. If you start with overcooked game the resulting dish may be dry. Try dishes such as satay, lasagne, kebabs and samosa. Game dishes using cooked game will freeze satisfactorily for 1-2 months (unless highly spiced) and a frozen bird can be safely cooked, made into a cooked dish and then frozen again.

FARMHOUSE GAME PIE
(Pictured opposite, recipe on page 128)

GAME LASAGNE
(Pictured below, recipe on page 129)

Game pie recipes

GAME PIE

A traditional game pie baked in a raised pie mould to serve cold. Hot-water crust pastry does not freeze well so it is best to make this pie fresh.

> **Approx 350g/12oz any cooked game, diced**
> **225g/8oz raw pie veal or lean boneless pork**
> **225g/8oz ham or bacon**
> **1 small onion, peeled**
> **Salt and pepper**
> **Good pinch of ground mace or nutmeg**
> *Pastry:*
> **450g/1lb plain flour**
> **1 level teaspoon salt**
> **100g/4oz lard**
> **200ml/7fl oz water or milk and water mixed**
> **Beaten egg to glaze**
> **2 level teaspoons powdered gelatine**
> **300ml/1/2 pint game stock (made from carcase)**

Mince the veal or pork, ham and onion into a bowl and mix in plenty of seasonings plus the mace or nutmeg.

For the pastry, sift the flour and salt into a bowl. Melt the lard in the water in a pan and then bring up to the boil. Pour the boiling liquid onto the flour, quickly mix to a dough and knead lightly until smooth. Roll about three-quarters of the pastry to a circle large enough to line a game pie mould or an 18-20cm/7-8in round cake tin, preferably with a loose base, or a 900g/2lb loaf tin; meanwhile cover the rest of the pastry with a cloth to keep it warm. Position the pastry in the lightly greased tin making sure it fits into the corners. Lay half the minced

meat in the tin, cover with the chopped game and then with the remaining mince. Roll out the remaining pastry for a lid, damp the edges and position. Press edges well together, trim and crimp. Use the trimmings to make leaves to decorate the top of the pie. Make a hole in the centre of the lid for the steam to escape. Stand the pie on a baking sheet and cook in a fairly hot oven (200°C/400°F, Gas Mark 6) for 30 minutes. Glaze the pie with beaten egg, reduce the temperature to moderate (160°C/325°F, Gas Mark 3) and cook for a further 30 minutes. Glaze again and continue for a further 30-45 minutes. If overbrowning lay a sheet of greaseproof paper over the pie.

Dissolve the gelatine in the stock, season well, and as the pie cools pour the liquid into it through a small funnel inserted in the central hole. Leave to rest and add more stock.

Chill thoroughly, preferably overnight before turning out. Garnish with salads.
SERVES 8-10

FARMHOUSE GAME PIE
(pictured on page 126)

A hot game pie layered with any game, sausage meat and mushrooms.

> **450g/1lb cooked game meat, diced (eg venison, hare, gamebirds)**
> **225g/8oz sausage meat**
> **100g/4oz fresh white breadcrumbs**
> **50g/2oz shredded suet**
> **Salt and pepper**
> **1 onion, peeled and finely chopped**
> **2 level tablespoons freshly chopped parsley**
> **2 level teaspoons freshly chopped thyme**

GAME PIE

FARMHOUSE GAME PIE

Grated rind of $^1/_2$ lemon

1 egg, beaten

100g/4oz mushrooms, chopped

Approx 200ml/7fl oz gravy or good
game stock

Pastry:

225g/8oz plain flour

50g/2oz lard or white fat

50g/2oz butter or margarine

Cold water to mix

Beaten egg or milk to glaze

Mix together the sausage meat,
breadcrumbs, suet, seasonings, onion,
parsley, thyme, lemon rind and egg.
Put half this mixture in the base of a
pie dish; cover with half the
mushrooms and the game, then the
remaining mushrooms and a final
layer of the forcemeat. Insert a pie
funnel in the middle and pour the
gravy or stock into the dish.

For the pastry, sift the flour and a
pinch of salt into a bowl, rub in the
fats until the mixture resembles fine
breadcrumbs and mix to a pliable
dough with cold water. Roll out the
pastry and cut a narrow strip to place
around the dampened rim of the pie
dish. Cover with a pastry lid after
brushing the strip with water. Press
well together and trim off the surplus
pastry. Knock up and crimp the edge
and use the pastry trimmings for
leaves to decorate the top of the pie.

Glaze with beaten egg or milk and
cook in a hot oven (200°C/400°F,
Gas Mark 6) for 20 minutes.
Reduce temperature to moderate
(180°C/350°F, Gas Mark 4) and
continue for about an hour, laying a
piece of greaseproof paper over the
pastry when sufficiently browned.
Serve hot.
SERVES 6

GAME LASAGNE

An old favourite with a difference.

225-275g/8-10oz cooked game meat,
coarsely minced

50g/2oz cooked ham or bacon,
minced

8-10 sheets green lasagne

Salt and pepper

3 tablespoons oil

1 large onion, peeled and chopped

1-2 cloves garlic, crushed

1 green pepper, deseeded and
chopped

200g/7oz can tomatoes

1 level tablespoon tomato purée

40g/1$^1/_2$oz butter or margarine

40g/1$^1/_2$oz flour

450ml/$^3/_4$ pint milk

1 level teaspoon dry mustard

75g/3oz mature Cheddar cheese,
grated

1 level tablespoon grated Parmesan
cheese

If lasagne is not pre-cooked, cook a
few sheets at a time in boiling salted
water to which 1 tablespoon oil has
been added until just tender – about
10 minutes. Drain on kitchen paper.

Fry the onion and garlic in the
remaining oil until soft, add the green
pepper and cook until lightly
browned. Stir in the mustard and
50g/2oz of the grated cheese. In a
fairly shallow, greased, ovenproof
dish arrange layers of lasagne, game
mixture and sauce, repeating them
and finishing with a layer of sauce.
Combine the remaining cheese with
the Parmesan and sprinkle over the
top. Bake in a fairly hot oven (200°C/
400°F, Gas Mark 6) for 40 minutes or
until golden brown and bubbling.
SERVES 4-5

GAME LASAGNE
(pictured on page 127)

Game pie recipes

GAME SAMOSA

These are Indian favourites, often eaten there as snacks, but they make excellent starters, or a tasty filling addition to a picnic or packed lunch. Smaller versions can be used as appetisers at cocktail parties.

Pastry:
225g/8oz plain flour
$^1/_2$ level teaspoon salt
4 tablespoons vegetable oil
4 tablespoons water
Little extra oil
Filling:
1 onion, peeled and finely chopped

1 clove garlic, crushed
4 tablespoons vegetable oil
$^1/_2$ fresh green chilli, deseeded and finely chopped
2 level teaspoons freshly grated raw root ginger
3 tablespoons water
3 level tablespoons finely chopped coriander or parsley
100g/4oz frozen peas
225g/8oz potatoes, boiled in their skins
175g/6oz cooked game, finely chopped or minced
1 level teaspoon ground coriander
1 level teaspoon ground cumin
Salt
2 tablespoons lemon juice
Vegetable oil for deep frying

For the pastry, sift the flour and salt into a bowl, add the oil and rub into the flour until it forms coarse breadcrumbs. Slowly add the water and work until it forms a stiff dough (you may need a little more water). Alternatively mix the dough in a food processor. Knead the dough for about 10 minutes then place in a well-oiled polythene bag and leave to rest for at least 30 minutes while making the filling.

For the filling, fry the onion and garlic in the oil until soft but only lightly coloured then add the chilli, ginger and water and bring to the boil. Add the coriander and peas and cook for 2-3 minutes. Peel the potatoes, dice and add to the pan with the game, spices, salt and lemon juice. Mix well and allow to cool.

Knead the pastry. Divide the mixture into 16 even-sized balls and roll out each one into a circle of approximately 10cm/4in or roll out

GAME SAMOSA
(pictured below)

the pastry and cut into rounds of approx 10cm/4in, re-rolling and cutting out more until all the pastry is used. Divide the filling between the circles, placing it at one side, dampen the edges of the pastry, fold over and press very tightly together.

Heat a pan of deep oil to moderately hot (about 190°C/375°F) and fry the samosas, a few at a time until they are golden brown all over, turning them several times. This should take about 3-4 minutes. Drain on absorbent kitchen paper and keep warm, or allow to cool.

Samosas will keep for 24 hours and can be reheated in a microwave oven set on high (100%) for about a minute.
MAKES ABOUT 16

MARY BERRY'S GAME PIE

A delicious cold pie which is Mary's favourite, the game can be altered to suit availability. This is ideal for using up the legs of game when the breasts have been removed for another recipe.

1 young pheasant (or other game , or 4 pheasant legs)
1.3kg/3lb roasting chicken
225g/8oz pork sausage meat
450g/1lb bacon pieces, derinded
1 small onion, peeled
1 level teaspoon grated nutmeg
2 level tablespoons freshly chopped parsley
1-2 level teaspoons salt
Freshly ground black pepper
8-10 eggs, hard-boiled (size 5 or 6)
Hot-water crust pastry:
550g/1¼lb plain flour
1 level teaspoon salt
125g/5oz lard
275ml/scant 9fl oz water or milk and water mixed

Beaten egg to glaze
1 level tablespoon powdered gelatine (15g/¹/₂oz packet)
1-2 tablespoons sherry

Mince the bacon and onion and put into a bowl. Remove the skin and bones from the birds and cut into small pieces. Add to the bowl with the sausage meat, nutmeg, parsley and seasonings and mix thoroughly.

Make the pastry as for Game Pie (see page 128). Use two-thirds to roll out and line a lightly greased 25cm/10in loose bottomed, round cake tin or pie mould. Place half the meat mixture in the pastry case, make 10 indents and add the eggs. Cover with the remaining meat mixture.

Roll out any trimmings of pastry thinly and chill, then cut out the letters to write 'game pie' and arrange on top of the pie attaching with beaten egg. Glaze the top of the pie thoroughly and make four holes for steam to escape. Stand on a baking sheet and cook in a hot oven (220°C/425°F, Gas Mark 7) for ³/₄ hour or until starting to brown.

Meanwhile use the game and chicken bones and skin to make a stock. Strain and reserve 300ml/¹/₂ pint. Reduce the oven temperature to cool (150°C/300°F, Gas Mark 2) and continue to cook for 2 hours. Remove and allow to cool.

Dissolve the gelatine in the stock, add the sherry and while the pie cools pour the liquid into it through the holes in the lid with the help of a small funnel. Chill overnight.

Remove from the tin and serve in wedges with salads.
SERVES 12

Game pie recipes

RAISED FARMHOUSE GAME PIE

Pheasant, chicken and bacon are the main flavourings for this pie made with roughly chopped game set in a jellied stock.

> 1 young pheasant, oven ready
> 2 chicken portions
> 225g/8oz streaky bacon rashers, derinded and chopped
> 1 small onion, peeled and finely chopped
> Salt and pepper
> 1 level tablespoon freshly chopped parsley
> 1/4 level teaspoon dried thyme
> 1/2 level teaspoon ground coriander
> Hot-water crust pastry (see Game Pie, page 128)
> 6 small hard-boiled eggs (optional)
> Beaten egg or milk to glaze
> 2 level teaspoons powdered gelatine
> 300ml/1/2 pint good stock

Strip all the meat off the pheasant and chicken portions and chop into small pieces. Add the bacon, onion, seasonings, parsley, thyme and coriander and mix well. Make up the pastry and roll out three-quarters of it.

Use to line a lightly greased 20-23cm/8-9in round cake tin or a 900g/2lb loaf tin (using a slightly smaller tin if omitting the eggs).

Spoon almost half of the filling into the pastry case then make 6 indents for the eggs and position them. Carefully cover with the rest of the filling – they must be completely covered.

Roll out the remaining pastry for a lid, damp the edges, position and press the edges firmly together. Trim and crimp and make one or two holes in the top. Decorate with leaves made from the pastry trimmings. Glaze the pie and cook in a fairly hot oven (200°C/400°F, Gas Mark 6) for 30 minutes. Glaze again and return to the oven reduced to moderate (180°C/350°F, Gas Mark 4) for 1 1/4-1 1/2 hours, laying a sheet of greaseproof paper over the pie when sufficiently browned.

Meanwhile use the game and chicken bones to make a stock and dissolve the gelatine in 300ml/1/2 pint of it. Season well and as the pie cools pour the stock into it through a funnel inserted in the holes in the lid. Chill thoroughly until set before removing from the tin.
SERVES 8-10

Note: not suitable to freeze because of the hot-water pastry.

PUFFY GAME PIE

A mixture of game to serve hot with a quick puff pastry which must be made and cooked immediately to get the puffy result. Any type of game or combinations of game can be used.

> 2 oven-ready grouse, quartered
> 1 oven-ready pheasant, cut into 6 or 8 pieces
> 1 large onion, peeled and sliced
> 2 carrots, peeled and sliced
> 1 bouquet garni
> Approx 600ml/1 pint stock
> Salt and pepper
> 25g/1oz butter or margarine
> 4 rashers streaky bacon, derinded and chopped
> 25g/1oz flour
> 100g/4oz mushrooms, sliced
> 200g/7oz sweetcorn kernels, drained

RAISED FARMHOUSE
GAME PIE

PUFFY GAME PIE

Quick Puff Pastry:
275g/10 oz plain flour
1 level teaspoon salt
225g/8oz block margarine or butter,
thoroughly chilled or semi-frozen
4-6 tablespoons iced water to mix
Beaten egg or milk to glaze

Put the pieces of grouse and pheasant into a saucepan with the onions, carrots, bouquet garni, stock and seasonings. Bring to the boil, cover and simmer gently for $3/4$-1 hour or until tender. Drain off the stock, discard the bouquet garni, and put the game and vegetables into a pie dish; leave to cool. Melt the butter in a pan, fry the bacon until crispy, then add the flour and cook for a minute or so. Gradually add 300ml/$1/2$ pint stock and bring to the boil. Add the mushrooms and sweetcorn, adjust the seasonings and pour over the game.

For the pastry, sift the flour and salt into a bowl. Coarsely grate the fat into the flour and mix lightly with a palate knife until evenly distributed. Add sufficient iced water to mix to a stiff dough. Do not knead. Turn onto a floured surface and either pat out to the size required or roll very gently using a well-floured rolling pin. Use the pastry to cover the pie, attaching to the dampened rim of the dish. Decorate with the trimmings and glaze. Make a hole in the centre and cook in a hot oven (220°C/425°F, Gas Mark 7) for about 40 minutes or until well browned and cooked through.
SERVES 6

GALANTINE OF GAME

Cooked grouse and pheasant are layered in a jellied wine stock together with a stuffing made from the rest of the carcase to give an ideal centrepiece for a cold buffet.

1 cooked pheasant
1 cooked grouse
225g/8oz minced raw pork or veal
Salt and pepper
1 onion, peeled and chopped
1 carrot, peeled and sliced
1 bay leaf or bouquet garni
15g/$1/2$oz packet powdered
gelatine
150ml/$1/4$ pint red wine
To garnish:
Salads

Carefully remove the breasts from the pheasant and grouse and strip off the skin. Strip off the rest of the meat from the carcases and mince, then mix with the pork or veal and season well. Put the carcases, skin, onion, carrot and bay leaf into a saucepan with $1/2$ litre/2 pints water, cover and simmer for 1-1$1/2$ hours to make a good stock. In a greased casserole or terrine layer slices of the breast of pheasant and grouse alternating with the minced mixture, seasoning each layer. Cover with foil or a lid and stand in a roasting tin containing 4cm/1$1/2$in water. Cook in a moderate oven (180°C/350°F, Gas Mark 4) for 50 minutes. Strain the stock and boil until reduced to 450ml/$3/4$ pint then dissolve the gelatine in it. Season and add the wine. Pour over the galantine until the dish is full. Cool then chill. Leave the remaining stock to set.

To serve, turn the galantine out carefully onto a serving dish or board. Garnish with salads and remaining jellied stock which should be chopped and placed around the galantine.
SERVES 6

Game pie recipes

GAME MOUSSE

Any cooked game can be used, but it is best if it is a well-flavoured variety or a bird that has been well hung.

225g/8oz cooked game, boneless
100g/4oz cooked ham
25g/1oz butter or margarine
25g/1oz flour
150ml/^{1}/$_4$ pint milk
Grated rind and juice of ^{1}/$_2$ lemon
Salt and pepper
1 level teaspoon dry mustard
Pinch of ground nutmeg
1 egg, beaten
2 tablespoons thick mayonnaise
3 level teaspoons powdered gelatine
2 tablespoons dry sherry
150ml/^{1}/$_4$ pint double cream
To garnish:
Cooked peas
Julienne strips of raw carrot

Mince the game and ham and set aside. Melt the fat in a pan, stir in the flour and cook for a minute or so, then gradually add the milk and bring up to the boil for 2 minutes, stirring continuously. Add the lemon rind and juice, seasonings, mustard, nutmeg and beaten egg followed by the mayonnaise. Dissolve the gelatine in the sherry in a basin over a pan of gently simmering water, or in a microwave.

Cool a little and then add to the sauce followed by the minced meats. Lightly whip the cream and fold through the mousse. Pour into a bowl and chill until set.

Decorate the top with cooked peas and carrot sticks and serve with salads.
SERVES 4-6

GAME SATAY

A variation on an Indonesian dish.

450g/1lb boned game (eg pheasant, wild duck, grouse, venison)
Marinade:
2 tablespoons dry sherry
1 tablespoon soy sauce
2 tablespoons sesame or safflower oil
grated rind and juice of ^{1}/$_2$ lemon
Salt and pepper
Sauce:
^{1}/$_2$ peeled onion, finely chopped
1 tablespoon sesame or safflower oil
100g/4oz crunchy peanut butter
1 level teaspoon brown sugar
2 teaspoons soy sauce
2 tablespoons tomato ketchup
^{1}/$_2$ level teaspoon chilli seasoning
Salt and pepper
6 tablespoons water or stock
1 level tablespoon sesame seeds

Cut game into small cubes or strips and put into a shallow dish. Combine all the ingredients for the marinade and pour over the game. Cover and marinate for 12-24 hours. For the sauce, fry the onion in the oil until very soft. Add the peanut butter, sugar, soy sauce, ketchup, chilli, seasonings, water and sesame seeds and bring slowly to the boil. Pour into a bowl and leave to cool.

Thread the pieces of drained game onto fine wooden or metal skewers and cook under a moderately hot grill for 3-4 minutes each side until well browned and just cooked through. Serve with rice and a green salad, or make into tiny satay on cocktail sticks and serve for cocktail snacks.
SERVES 4

GAME MOUSSE

GAME SATAY
(pictured opposite)

GAME CROQUETTES

The game can be of any type or a mixture of several types of game.

**175-225g/6-8oz cooked game meat
or trimmings from carcases
1 onion, peeled
2 slices cooked ham or 3 rashers
lean bacon
225g/8oz sausage meat
1 tablespoon freshly chopped
parsley
Salt and pepper
25g/1oz fresh breadcrumbs
Pinch of ground mace or nutmeg
1 egg, beaten
Dry or golden breadcrumbs
Shallow fat or oil for frying**

To garnish:
Watercress

Mince the game, onion and ham or bacon. Add to the sausage meat with the parsley, seasonings, breadcrumbs, mace or nutmeg and the beaten egg. Mix thoroughly, then divide into eight and shape into croquettes or flat cakes. Coat evenly in breadcrumbs and fry in shallow fat for 4-5 minutes each side or until well browned and cooked through. Keep warm. Meanwhile make one of the sauces (see over) to serve with the croquettes.

Garnish with watercress and serve.
SERVES 4

See over for sauces

GAME CROQUETTES

Game pie recipes

Special tomato sauce:

Put 150ml/^{1}/4 pint each of tomato ketchup and red or white wine into a saucepan with a crushed clove of garlic, and seasonings. Bring to the boil and simmer uncovered for about 5 minutes or until thickened, stirring frequently. Add 50-100g/2-4oz chopped mushrooms and continue to cook for 2-3 minutes. Serve hot.

Curried mayonnaise:

Mix together 150ml/^{1}/4 pint thick mayonnaise with 4 tablespoons soured cream or natural yoghurt and 1-2 level teaspoons curry powder, 1 level teaspoon snipped chives and a little grated lemon rind.

JELLIED GAME MOUSSE

An attractive jellied mousse with layers of vegetables and game.

> 275g/10oz cooked game (any type)
> 100g/4oz cooked ham
> 40g/ 1^1/2oz butter
> 3 level tablespoons flour
> 450ml/^{3}/4 pint milk
> Salt and pepper
> 550ml/1 pint aspic jelly
> 15g/^{1}/2oz powdered gelatine
> 4 tablespoons water
> 4 tablespoons single or soured cream
> 225g/8 oz packet frozen chopped spinach, cooked
> *To garnish*
> Sliced hard-boiled egg
> Sliced tomato and salads

Lightly grease a round cake tin approx 20cm/8in in diameter, preferably with a loose base. Melt the butter in a pan, stir in the flour and cook for 1 minute. Gradually add the milk and bring up to the boil, stirring frequently. Simmer for 2 minutes, season well and remove from the heat. Pour half the sauce into a bowl, add 150ml/^{1}/4 pint liquid aspic jelly and leave until on the point of setting.

Finely chop or mince the ham with 100g/4oz of the cooked game and fold through the sauce. Pour into the tin and chill until set. Dissolve the gelatine in the water in a bowl over a pan of gently simmering water, or in a microwave, add to the remaining sauce together with the cream and mix well. Squeeze the excess water from the spinach, fold through the sauce and spoon over the set layer in the tin. Chill until set.

Cut the remaining game into strips and lay over the spinach layer in the tin. Cover with aspic and chill until set. Carefully remove from the tin and place on a serving dish. Decorate the top with slices of hard-boiled egg and tomato and arrange salads around. SERVES 8-10

VENISON PIE

Any cut of venison suitable to casserole can be used for this dish.

> 675g/1^1/2lb venison, cut into 2.5cm/1in cubes
> 25g/1oz seasoned flour
> 2 tablespoons oil or dripping
> 1 onion, peeled and chopped
> 100g/4oz streaky bacon rashers, derinded and chopped
> 150ml/^{1}/4 pint red or white wine
> 600ml/1 pint stock
> Salt and pepper
> 6-8 juniper berries, crushed
> 2 level tablespoons coarse orange marmalade
> 4 tablespoons cream

Suet crust pastry:
225g/8oz self-raising flour
1/2 level teaspoon salt
75-100g/3-4oz shredded suet
Approx 150ml/1/4 pint cold water
Beaten egg or milk to glaze

Toss the venison in the seasoned flour, then fry in the heated fat until well sealed. Add the onion and bacon and continue to cook for a few minutes. Sprinkle in any remaining flour, mix well, then add the wine and stock and bring up to the boil. Season well, add the juniper berries and marmalade and cover the pan. Simmer gently for about 1 1/2 hours or until tender. Adjust the seasonings, stir in the cream, and pour into a pie dish with a funnel in the centre. Cool.

For the pastry, sift the flour and salt into a bowl and mix in the suet. Add sufficient water to mix to a firm but pliable dough. Roll out the pastry on a well-floured surface, about 2.5cm/1in larger than the top of the dish. Cut off a strip 2.5cm/1in wide and place on the dampened rim of the dish. Brush this with water and then position the lid, pressing the edges well together. Trim the edges and crimp. Use the trimmings to make leaves to decorate the top of the pie. Make a hole in the centre and glaze thoroughly with beaten egg or milk.

Bake in a fairly hot oven (200ºC/400ºF, Gas Mark 6) for 35-45 minutes until the crust is a good golden brown and crisp and the filling piping hot.
SERVES 4-6

Note: suet-crust is not the best pastry to freeze but the filling will freeze well for up to 2 months.

VENISON PASTIES

Tasty snacks to serve hot or cold.

450g/1lb venison (from the haunch or saddle, if possible)
1-2 onions, peeled and chopped
450ml/3/4 pint stock
150ml/1/4 pint red wine
Salt and pepper
1 bouquet garni
2 tablespoons redcurrant jelly
1 level teaspoon cornflour
350g/12oz shortcrust pastry (made using 350g/12oz plain flour etc)
1 level teaspoon freshly chopped mixed herbs or parsley
Beaten egg or milk to glaze

Cut the venison into small dice and place in a saucepan with the onions, stock, wine, seasonings, bouquet garni and jelly. Bring to the boil, cover and simmer until the meat is tender, about 45 minutes. Strain off the liquor, return it to a clean pan and boil hard until reduced to about 200ml/1/3 pint; then thicken with the cornflour blended in 1 tablespoon cold water and bring back to the boil. Roll out the pastry and cut into six 15cm/6in circles. Place a portion of meat and onions on one side of each pastry round and sprinkle each with chopped herbs or parsley. Damp the edges of each pastry circle and fold over the filling to enclose. Press all the edges firmly together and crimp. Place the pasties on a greased baking sheet and glaze with beaten egg or milk. Make a slit in the top of each pasty and bake in a fairly hot oven (200ºC/400ºF, Gas Mark 6) for about 30 minutes. Reheat the sauce and pour a little into each pasty through the slit using a funnel.
SERVES 6

VENISON PASTIES

PÂTÉS AND TERRINES
FOR ALL TYPES OF GAME

GAME pâtés and terrines make very popular starters. They are widely used to serve with salads for lunch or supper, as part of a buffet spread and for all types of snack as well as on picnics, not to mention as excellent sandwich fillings.

The French word pâté means a savoury pie. This meaning has been extended by us to cover what we now know as pâté by the ingredients being minced and/or pounded to make a type of paste which is then often made in a pie shape or in a pie tin and cooked in a terrine. This dish is usually earthenware, often oval and about 7.5 cm/3in deep and the cooked terrine is served from the dish; while a pâté is more often turned out and served with salads.

All types of game, feathered and furred, can be used for both pâté and terrines. Fish can also be used. Often gamefish such as salmon or trout are mixed with other types of white fish for terrines.

A more tasty pâté will result if the game has been well hung. The texture can be smooth, coarse or in between, according to preference. Sometimes whole breasts of game are layered with the pâté mixture to give an interesting appearance as well as mixed flavours and textures. In some pâtés the ingredients are minced raw and then cooked in the tin; with others the ingredients are part-cooked with wine and flavourings and then minced mixed with beaten eggs and baked while some are first marinated before any mincing or chopping is done.

A water bath or roasting tin containing 4-5 cm/1^1/2-2in water is recommended for cooking both pâtés and terrines as it prevents drying out during cooking. A pâté should be weighted as it cools to give a good shape and even texture. Cover a piece of wood or thick card a little smaller than the top of the cooking container with foil and then put onto the pâté with a piece of greaseproof paper between it and the pâté, and top it with scale weights, a brick or heavy cans of food.

Game pâtés and terrines can be frozen for up to 2 months. Turn a pâté out of the cooking container and wrap first in greaseproof paper and then foil (if foil alone is used the acids from the pâté may eat into the foil). A terrine can be covered with greaseproof paper and foil but is usually left in its terrine. Thaw out slowly and completely before use. Do not add aspic jelly until thawed out as it does not freeze well.

COUNTRY GAME PÂTÉ
(pictured opposite, recipe on page 142)

HARE AND PIGEON TERRINE
(pictured below, recipe on page 143)

Pâté and terrine recipes

POTTED GAME

Any type of cooked game can be used for this recipe.

225g/8oz cooked game, boneless
100g/4oz butter
1 onion, peeled and very finely chopped or minced
1-2 cloves garlic, crushed
2 tablespoons sherry or port
Approx 4 tablespoons good stock
Salt and freshly ground black pepper
Pinch of ground mace or nutmeg
Pinch of dried mixed herbs (optional)
To garnish:
Sprigs of fresh herbs and tomatoes

Mince the cooked game finely, twice or process finely in a food processor. Melt half the butter in a pan and fry the onion and garlic gently until soft and only just lightly coloured. Stir in the minced meat followed by the sherry and just enough stock to moisten. Season to taste with salt, pepper, mace and herbs if used. Press the game mixture into a lightly greased dish or several small dishes and level the tops. Chill until firm. Melt the remaining butter and pour a thin layer over the potted game. Add a few sprigs of fresh herbs and chill thoroughly so the herbs set in the butter. Serve garnished with tomato slices or cherry tomatoes and crusty bread. Potted game may also be used to fill sandwiches. It will keep in the refrigerator for 2-3 days but no longer as it does not contain any preservative.
SERVES 6

Note: suitable to freeze for up to 1 month.

GAME PÂTÉ

This recipe is good for badly shot pheasants or other birds.

225g/8oz boned raw game
150ml/$^1/_4$ pint red wine
2 bay leaves
8 black peppercorns
2 cloves garlic, crushed
2 tablespoons oil
1 thinly sliced onion
225g/8oz boneless belly pork, skinned
100 g/4oz streaky bacon, derinded
225g/8oz chicken livers
1 slice white bread
1 egg
Salt and pepper
Good pinch of ground nutmeg, mace or allspice
1 level tablespoon chopped mixed fresh herbs
To garnish:
Aspic jelly
Black olives
Sprigs of fresh herbs

Put the game cut into small pieces into a bowl with the wine, bay leaves, peppercorns, garlic, oil and onion, mix well, cover and leave to marinate overnight or at least for 3-4 hours.

Pick out the pieces of meat from the marinade and mince (fine or coarse) with the pork, streaky bacon and chicken livers. Soak the bread in the strained marinade, then mash up finely or put through the mincer with the meats. Mix all the minced meats together adding the remaining marinade, egg, seasonings, nutmeg and herbs. Place in a well-greased 1 litre/2 pint terrine or ovenproof casserole, cover with greased foil, greaseproof paper or a lid and stand in a roasting tin with water coming halfway up the side of the container.

Cook in a moderate oven (180°C/350°F, Gas Mark 4) for 1¹/₂-2 hours or until the juices run clear when pierced with a fine skewer. Cool then chill thoroughly. If liked cover with a layer of liquid aspic, setting halved black olives and sprigs of fresh herbs into it.
SERVES 8

Note: suitable to freeze for up to 2 months without the aspic jelly.

HUNTER'S PÂTÉ
Breasts of game are needed here.

225g/8oz pork sausagement
225g/8oz pheasant or other gamebird breasts, skinned
450g/1lb venison, coarsely minced
100g/4oz streaky bacon in a piece, minced
1 onion, peeled and minced
1-2 cloves garlic, crushed
¹/₂ level teaspoon ground mace
Salt and pepper
3-4 tablespoons brandy, whisky or wine
1 egg, beaten
Approx 175g/6oz streaky bacon rashers, derinded

Put the sausage meat into a bowl. Cut the breasts of game into thin strips and add to the bowl with the venison, minced bacon, onion, garlic, mace and seasonings and bind together with the brandy and egg. Stretch the bacon rashers with the back of a knife and use to line a large well-greased loaf tin. Add the minced mixture and fold over the ends of the bacon. Cover with greased foil or greaseproof paper and stand in a roasting tin with about

2.5cm/1in water in it. Cook in a moderate oven (180°C/350°F, Gas Mark 4) for about 2 hours or until the juices run clear when pierced with a skewer. Cool thoroughly and then chill overnight. Turn out and garnish.
SERVES 10

Note: suitable to freeze for up to 2 months.

FRESH SALMON PÂTÉ
A good use for left-over salmon.

225g/8oz cooked salmon
2 level tablespoons finely chopped onion or spring onions
50g/2oz butter or margarine
¹/₂ teaspoon grated lemon rind
Approx 2 teaspoons lemon juice
Salt and pepper
Little garlic powder
1 level teaspoon freshly chopped tarragon or dill (optional)
2-3 tablespoons double or soured cream
To garnish:
Black olives and lemon wedges
Mixed lettuce leaves

Flake the salmon finely, discarding any skin and bones. Fry the onion in the butter until just soft, and then beat into the salmon with the lemon rind and juice. Season with salt, pepper and a pinch of garlic powder and then add the herbs. Add sufficient cream or soured cream to bind together. If necessary add a little more lemon juice to sharpen. Put into individual dishes or one larger dish and chill. Garnish with olives, lemon and lettuce leaves.
SERVES 4

Note: suitable to freeze for up to 1 month

HUNTER'S PÂTÉ

FRESH SALMON PÂTÉ

Pâté and terrine recipes

PHEASANT AND LIVER PÂTÉ

A coarse pâté, the pheasant must be fairly 'high' for the best flavour.

1/2 **raw high pheasant or two legs of pheasant**
350g/12oz pig's liver
350g/12oz streaky bacon rashers, derinded
1 large onion, peeled
2 cloves garlic, crushed
1 egg, beaten
3-4 tablespoons brandy or port
Salt and black pepper
2 bay leaves
To garnish:
Salads

Strip the meat from the bones and mince reasonably finely with the liver, half the bacon and the onion. Add the garlic, egg, brandy or port and plenty of seasonings. Stretch the bacon rashers with the back if a knife and use to line a greased 900g/2lb loaf tin with the bay leaves in the base of it. Spoon in the pâté mixture folding over the ends of the bacon to partly cover it. Stand the tin in a roasting tin containing about 4cm/1^1/2in water and cook in a moderate oven (180°C/350°F, for about 1^1/2 hours. Remove the tin from the water bath, cool a little then cover with grease-proof paper and a weight. When cold, refrigerate for several hours. Turn out and serve in slices with salads and with hot toast or French bread.
SERVES 6-8

Note: this pâté will freeze for up to 2 months if well wrapped in clingfilm and then foil.

COUNTRY GAME PÂTÉ

(pictured on page 138)

A smooth pâté which is made and served in the same ovenproof dish.

450g/1lb raw boned game (eg hare, gamebird, venison or a mixture)
350g/12oz pig's liver
175g/6oz streaky bacon, derinded
1 large onion, peeled and chopped
50g/2oz butter or margarine
1-2 cloves garlic, crushed
4 tablespoons port, brandy or red wine
1/2 **level teaspoon ground ginger**
1 level tablespoon freshly chopped parsley
Salt and black pepper
2 eggs, beaten
To garnish:
Sliced cucumber
Tomatoes

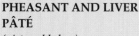

PHEASANT AND LIVER PÂTÉ
(pictured below)

COUNTRY GAME PÂTÉ

Stuffed green olives
Aspic jelly (optional)

Mince the liver, raw game, bacon
and onion. Melt the butter in a pan
and fry the minced mixture and garlic
until sealed, about 5 minutes, stirring
frequently. Cool slightly then if a
smoother pâté is required either mince
the mixture or process in a food
processor. Add the port, brandy or
wine and all the other ingredients to
the minced meats and mix thoroughly.
Pour into a well-greased ovenproof
dish and cover with buttered
greaseproof paper and either a lid or
foil. Stand in a roasting tin containing
about 4cm/1^1/2in water and cook in a
moderate oven (160°C/325°F, Gas
Mark 3) for 1^1/2 hours, removing the
foil and covering for the last 15
minutes. Cool and chill the pâté
thoroughly. Garnish the top with
slices of cucumber, tomato and stuffed
olives and, if liked, add a thin layer of
aspic jelly. Chill again and serve the
pâté spooned from the dish or turn out
onto a board and garnish with salads.
SERVES 8-10

Note: suitable to freeze for up to 2
months without the garnish.

HARE AND PIGEON TERRINE
(pictured on page 139)
The layers in this terrine show
beautifully when sliced.

1 hare or large rabbit, skinned
and paunched
4 pigeon breasts, taken from
2 whole pigeons
5-6 tablespoons dry white wine
6 whole black peppercorns
Bay leaves

1-2 cloves garlic, crushed
225g/8oz lean raw pork
1 onion, peeled
1 level teaspoon dried oregano
Salt and black pepper
8-10 rashers streaky bacon,
derinded
To garnish:
Salads

Remove the meat from the hare or
rabbit (approx 675g/1^1/2lb) and place
in a bowl with the pigeon breasts.
Pour the wine overall, add the
peppercorns, one bay leaf and the
garlic and leave to marinate for 2-3
hours in a cool place. Drain off the
marinade, strain and retain. Take out
the smaller pieces of hare or rabbit
(approx 550g/1^1/4lb) and mince with
the pork and onion; then add the
oregano, seasonings and marinade.
Stretch out the rashers of bacon with
the back of a knife and use to line a
greased terrine dish or a loaf tin.

Fill the base with the minced meats
and then add a layer of pigeon breast
and hare or rabbit meat. Continue
adding layers until all the meat is used
up. Cover with greased greaseproof
paper and then the lid of the terrine or
a piece of foil and stand in a roasting
tin containing about 4cm/1^1/2in
water. Cook in a moderately hot oven
(190°C/375°F, Gas Mark 5) for
1^1/4-1^1/2 hours or until the juices run
clear when pierced with a skewer.
Leave to cool in the container with a
weight on top and then chill for at
least 2 hours and preferably overnight.
Turn out and garnish with salads.
SERVES 6-8

Note: suitable to freeze for up to 2
months.

**HARE AND PIGEON
TERRINE**

Pâté and terrine recipes

WILD DUCK TERRINE

A good flavoured terrine with a smooth and chunky texture.

450g/1lb wild duck breasts
50g/2oz butter or margarine
350g/12oz belly pork, skinned
350g/12oz pie veal
75g/3oz streaky bacon, derinded
150ml/$\frac{1}{4}$pint white wine
1 clove garlic, crushed
Salt and pepper
1 orange, thinly sliced
Approx 250ml/8fl oz aspic jelly
Fresh bay leaves

Remove the breasts from the ducks (you will need about six breasts) and sauté lightly in the butter for about 10 minutes or until partly cooked.

Trim surplus fat from the pork and mince with the pie veal and all but two of the rashers of bacon. Add the wine, garlic and plenty of seasonings. Dice the duck. Put half the minced mixture in a well-greased terrine or casserole, add the duck meat and cover with the remaining mince. Cut the bacon rashers into narrow strips and arrange these in a lattice over the pâté. Cover completely with foil and stand in a roasting tin containing at least 2.5cm/1in water. Cook in a moderate oven (160°C/325°F, Gas Mark 3) for $1\frac{1}{2}$-2 hours. Remove from the water bath, cool and then chill. Decorate the top with orange slices dipped into liquid aspic jelly and then cover with a layer of aspic. Chill and serve garnished with fresh bay leaves. SERVES 10

Note: suitable to freeze for 6-8 weeks, but without the orange garnish and aspic. Add this when thawed.

VENISON PÂTÉ

The liver of the venison is the coveted prize usually given to or taken by the stalker who kills the animal. It make a very good pâté if you are lucky enough to get hold of a small amount.

225g/8oz venison liver, roughly chopped
100g/4oz butter
2 level tablespoons finely chopped onion
2 rashers bacon, derinded and chopped
1 clove garlic, crushed
2-3 tablespoons brandy
Salt and freshly ground black pepper
Pinch of ground allspice
2-3 tablespoons double cream
To garnish:
Cucumber slices
Stuffed olives

Melt half the butter in a pan and fry the onion, bacon and garlic gently until soft. Add the liver and fry gently for about 5 minutes, stirring frequently until just cooked through. Add the brandy and plenty of seasonings and the allspice. Cool a little and then either liquidise, pureé in a food processor or mince finely. Add the cream, adjust seasonings and turn into a serving dish. Level the top, then cool and chill. Cover with a layer of melted butter and chill again. Garnish with cucumber and olives and serve with fingers of toast or crispbreads. SERVES 4-6

RABBIT TERRINE

This makes an excellent starter or a good cold cutting terrine to serve with salads.

100g/4oz boneless belly pork, skinned and cubed
100g/4oz pig's liver, sliced into strips
1 onion, peeled
1-2 cloves garlic, crushed
450g/1lb boneless raw rabbit
Salt and pepper
1/4 level teaspoon ground coriander
2 level tablespoons freshly chopped parsley
1 level tablespoon freshly chopped basil or 1 level teaspoon dried basil
4 tablespoons wine (red or white)
1 egg, beaten
To garnish:
Salads

Put the pork into a pan and fry gently until the fat runs; add the liver and cook for a few minutes until well sealed. Cool.

Mince the pork, liver, onion, garlic and rabbit either finely or more coarsely, according to taste. Season well and beat in the coriander, parsley, basil, wine and beaten egg. Turn either into a well-greased 450-675g/1-1½lb loaf tin or a terrine or casserole dish and cover with greased foil. Stand the terrine in a roasting tin with water coming halfway up the sides of the dish. Cook in a moderate oven (180°C/350°F, Gas Mark 4) for 1½ hours or until the juices run clear when pierced with a skewer. Cool, then chill overnight and serve turned out of the tin or still in the terrine or casserole dish.

Garnish with salads or with gherkin fans and stuffed olives. Serve with hot toast, crackers, rolls or crusty bread and butter or in slices with salads.
SERVES 6-8

SMOKED TROUT PÂTÉ

This is a delicately flavoured pâté which can be made with your own home-smoked trout or commercially prepared ones.

350g/12oz boned smoked trout
50g/2oz butter
75g/3oz fresh white breadcrumbs
Finely grated rind and juice of 1 lemon
Salt and black pepper
Good pinch of ground nutmeg or mace
150ml/¼ pint single cream
Approx 200ml/8fl oz aspic jelly (optional)
Sprigs of fresh fennel, dill or parsley

Flake the trout flesh finely into a bowl, discarding any skin and bones. Melt the butter in a pan or in the microwave set on medium and then stir in the breadcrumbs, lemon rind and juice and mix thoroughly.

Add this to the flaked trout and season well. Fold the cream through the mixture and divide between 6 individual ramekin or soufflé dishes, or put into one larger dish, level the tops and chill.

If liked make up the aspic jelly and leave until on the point of setting. Pour or spoon a layer over the pâté, setting a leaf of fennel, dill or parsley into it. Chill until set.

Alternatively simply garnish with herbs and stuffed olives.
SERVES 5-6

Note: can be frozen for up to 1 month, but do not add the layer of aspic until thawed out.

SMOKED TROUT PÂTÉ

GAME SOUPS
FOR EVERY OCCASION

GAME IS one of the best ingredients for soup making. Indeed the carcases or bones of any game, whether cooked or raw, make a very good stock suitable to use as the base for any soups. A recipe for game stock is given in the consommé recipe (page 148) and this can be used as it is or similarly for all game stock. You really need one carcase of a pheasant or two of grouse or other small birds to 1.2-1.75litres/2-3pints water plus some root vegetables (but not potatoes) and herbs if liked. Salt is not added until the stock is actually used in a recipe. A bouquet garni is often added for flavour to stocks and soups. It is simply a small bunch of fresh herbs tied in a small piece of muslin (for easy removal) which is left in the stock, soup or casserole throughout cooking. Tie a sprig of parsley, thyme and a bay leaf in a piece of muslin adding 4-5 black peppercorns, 1-2 whole cloves and, if liked, a small blade of mace.

Stock will keep in the refrigerator for 3-4 days but it should be boiled up each day and then rapidly cooked and chilled again. It will also freeze satisfactorily for 2-3 months either as it is or in a concentrated form made by boiling the stock in an open pan until reduced by half. It can then be made up to its original strength when required but will take up less freezer space for storage.

All liquids, whether stock or soup, must have a headspace of about 2.5cm/1in left in the container when freezing, for all liquids expand during the freezing process and will burst out of whatever they are frozen in if this is omitted. Use rigid plastic containers or stand polythene bags in jugs or basins and fill up and freeze in the jugs; remove the bags from the jugs when solid and secure tightly.

For small quantities of stock freeze in ice cube trays and then pack in polythene bags. Remember to label clearly. Most soups also freeze well but do not add ingredients such as cream, yoghurt or eggs until thawed. Also if there is a certain amount of milk to be added to the soup, this should be left until it is thawed, for it will save space in the container and consequently the freezer. Most soups will store well for 2-3 months, but strong-flavoured ones and fish soups are best stored for only 4-8 weeks, especially when using smoked fish. Do not freeze jellied consommé.

Garnishes add the final touch to a soup and are easy to make. Try toasted croutons – slices of bread lightly toasted and cut into small cubes; or fried croutons – cubes of bread fried in a mixture of oil and butter or margarine; grated orange or lemon rind; or julienne strips of orange or lemon rind removed from the fruit with a potato peeler, cut into narrow strips and blanched in boiling water for 5 minutes; chopped parsley and/or chives and/or other fresh herbs; leaves of herbs, eg dill, mint, coriander etc; thinly pared strips of carrot; grated hard-boiled egg; crisply fried and crumbled bacon rinds or streaky bacon; swirls of single, double or soured cream or natural yoghurt and grated cheese are just a few.

Soups are ideal for snack lunches, in a flask for a picnic, snug suppers by the fire with hot crusty bread or for the first course of a meal; and, of course, many can be served chilled as well as piping hot.

**CREAM OF
PHEASANT AND
TARRAGON SOUP**
*(pictured opposite,
recipe on page 151)*

Game soups

GAME CONSOMMÉ

A traditional clear game soup suitable to serve before any meal.

Stock:
**Carcase of 2 pheasants or wild
ducks or 3-4 partridges or grouse or
1.8kg/4lb venison bones
1-2 onions, peeled and sliced
2 carrots, peeled and sliced
2 sticks celery, sliced
1 bay leaf
2.25 litres/4 pints water**
Consommé:
**225g/8oz lean beef, minced
1 carrot, peeled and chopped
1 large onion, peeled and roughly
chopped
1 bouquet garni
Whites and shells of 2 eggs
Salt and pepper
1 tablespoon port or sherry
(optional)
Few julienne strips of cooked
celery and carrot and/or 25g/1oz
cooked miniature pasta shapes**

For the stock, put all the ingredients into a large saucepan and bring up to the boil. Remove any scum from the surface, then cover the pan and simmer gently for $1^1/2$-2 hours. Give an occasional stir and press the carcase to break up the bones during cooking. Cool a little then strain through a fine sieve.

Put a generous litre/2 pints of the stock into a clean saucepan with the beef and leave to soak for an hour or so. Add the carrot, onion, bouquet garni, whites and crushed shells of the eggs and plenty of seasonings. Heat the pan, whisking continuously until nearly boiling, then bring to the boil, undisturbed. Simmer very gently for about an hour, taking care not to break the frothy layer on the top. Pour through a jelly bag or scalded cloth, keeping the froth back until last; then pour through the filter of egg in the cloth again. Repeat until clear; then return to a clean pan. Adjust seasonings if necessary, but take care not to cloud the soup.

A little port or sherry may be added if liked and add the strips of carrot and celery and/or pasta shapes.

Serve hot with breadsticks or melba toast.
SERVES 4-6

JELLIED GAME CONSOMMÉ

This soup is best if only lightly jellied. It can be set firmer if preferred by increasing the gelatine content.

**1 recipe quantity hot game
consommé (see Game Consommé)
2-3 level teaspoons powdered
gelatine**
To garnish:
Julienne strips of orange rind

The better the stock, the less gelatine will be required. Dissolve the gelatine in about 4 tablespoons of the consommé in a bowl over a pan of hot water. Stir through the rest of the consommé, cool and then chill thoroughly until set.

The consommé should have a light set, just enough so it can be roughly chopped or broken up with a spoon. Serve in soup bowls topped with strips of orange rind which have been cooked in boiling water for 5 minutes, rinsed under boiling water and drained thoroughly. The orange rind can also be set into the consommé.
SERVES 4-6

GAME CONSOMMÉ

JELLIED GAME
CONSOMMÉ

GAME SOUP

This is a recipe which makes a good soup whether using hare, pheasant or venison, or even a mixture of game.

225g/8oz raw or cooked game (hare, pheasant, venison etc)
900ml/1^1/2pints good game stock (see Game Consommé recipe)
1-1^1/2 level teaspoons dried mixed herbs
Pinch of ground mace
2 anchovy fillets (optional)
25g/1oz butter or margarine
25g/1oz flour
4 tablespoons sherry
1 level tablespoon redcurrant, cranberry or rowan jelly
Juice of ^{1}/2 lemon
Salt and pepper
Gravy browning (optional)
To garnish:
Fried croutons

If using raw game put into a saucepan with 300ml/^{1}/2pint of the stock, the herbs and mace. Bring to the boil, cover and simmer gently until soft. Remove the meat (or use the cooked game) and mince finely with the anchovies, or chop finely in a food processor. Make the stock up to 300ml/^{1}/2 pint with water if necessary, and strain back into the remainder.

Melt the fat in a pan, stir in the flour and cook for a minute or so. Gradually add the stock and bring to the boil, stirring continuously.

Add the minced game, sherry, redcurrant jelly, lemon juice and seasonings to taste; simmer for 4-5 minutes.

Adjust the seasonings and, if liked, add just a touch of gravy browning to increase the colour. Serve hot, garnished with croutons.
SERVES 4-6

Note: suitable to freeze for up to 2 months.

GAME-A-LEEKIE SOUP

Even better when made with game than with the traditional chicken.

1 pheasant or 2 partridges or grouse, oven ready
1.2-2.25 litres/2-4 pints water or stock
4 leeks, trimmed, thinly sliced and washed
1 onion, peeled and thinly sliced
2 carrots, peeled and diced (optional)
Salt and pepper
1 bouquet garni
12 prunes, soaked if necessary
To garnish:
Chopped parsley

Place the gamebirds in a saucepan with the washed giblets if they are available and the water, leeks, onion, carrots (if used), seasonings and bouquet garni. Bring up to the oil and remove any scum that forms. Cover and simmer very gently for 2^1/2-3 hours until the meat simply falls off the birds. Add the prunes and continue cooking for about 15 minutes. Remove the bouquet garni and carefully lift out the birds. Spoon off any fat from the surface of the soup and adjust the seasonings. Chop as much of the game flesh as you like, keeping it free of skin, gristle and bone and return it to the soup. Reheat and serve very hot sprinkled with parsley.
SERVES 6-8

GAME SOUP

GAME-A-LEEKIE SOUP

Game soup recipes

SALMON BISQUE
A good filling soup ideal for picnics.

1-2 salmon heads (depending on size) or a tail piece of salmon weighing approx 450g/1lb
900ml/1¹/₂ pints water
1 bay leaf
1 lemon sliced
Few black peppercorns
25g/1oz butter or margarine
2 level tablespoons finely chopped onion or spring onions
25g/1oz flour
150ml/¹/₄pint dry white wine or fish stock
150ml/¹/₄pint single or double cream
Salt and pepper
To garnish:
Freshly chopped fennel and/or chives

Put the salmon into a saucepan with the water, bay leaf, lemon and peppercorns. Bring to the boil, remove scum, then cover the pan and simmer gently for 20 minutes. Remove from the heat, strain the stock and reserve 600ml/1pint. Discard all the skin and bones from the salmon and flake the flesh, removing all the pieces from the head, if used. Melt the fat in a pan and sauté the onion gently for about 5 minutes. Stir in the flour, cook for 1 minute then gradually add the stock and wine and bring to the boil. Add the flaked salmon and season to taste; simmer for 3-4 minutes. Add the cream and reheat gently. Serve hot or chilled topped with chopped fennel, dill or chives or simply lay a sprig of fennel or dill on the surface.
SERVES 6

Note: Suitable to freeze for up to 1 month, but add the cream when thawed and reheated.

SMOKED TROUT CHOWDER
Fish soups are more and more popular and are both quick and easy to make. This recipe uses smoked trout but can also be made using smoked salmon trimmings.

450g/1lb smoked trout check
2 onions, peeled and thinly sliced
50g/2oz butter or margarine
3 carrots, peeled and very finely chopped
2 sticks celery, finely chopped
2 level tablespoons flour
1.1 litres/2 pints chicken stock or half stock and half water
225g/¹/₂lb potatoes, peeled and diced
150ml/¹/₄pint single cream

SALMON BISQUE
(pictured below)

SMOKED TROUT CHOWDER

Salt and pepper
4 level tablespoons freshly
chopped parsley

Remove the heads, skin and bones from the trout and flake the flesh finely. Fry the onions very gently in the melted fat for 2-3 minutes. Add the carrots and celery and fry very gently for 4-5 minutes until soft but not coloured. Stir in the flour, cook for 1 minute, then gradually add the stock and bring up to the boil. Add the potatoes and simmer gently for 2-3 minutes. Adjust the seasonings stir in the cream and 3 tablespoons of the parsley and heat to just below boiling. Serve garnished with the rest of the parsley and serve with hot crusty bread and butter.
SERVES 4-5

Note: For smoked salmon soup use 175g/6oz salmon pieces or trimmings and 350g/12oz white fish fillets in place of the trout. Poach the white fish in the stock, remove skin and flake; strain the stock and continue as above.

These soups are suitable to freeze for up to a month, but add the cream when thawed and reheated.

CREAM OF PHEASANT AND TARRAGON SOUP
(pictured on page 146)

A really good creamy soup to serve as a warming snack. It will freeze well so it can be served when pheasant is out of season. If you have no tarragon, try using dill, basil or parsley instead.

1-2 pheasant carcases, raw or
cooked
Generous litre/2 pints water
50g/2oz butter or margarine

1 large onion, peeled and finely
chopped
50g/2oz flour
Salt and freshly ground black
pepper
$^{1}/_{2}$ level teaspoon celery salt
$^{1}/_{4}$ level teaspoon ground
coriander
300ml/$^{1}/_{2}$ pint milk
150ml/$^{1}/_{4}$ single cream
3 level tablespoons freshly
chopped tarragon
To garnish;
Fried croutons or sprigs of tarragon

Put the pheasant carcase into a saucepan with the water. Bring to the boil, cover and simmer for about $1^{1}/_{2}$ hours. Drain and reserve the stock. Remove about 50-75g/2-3oz pheasant meat trimmings from the carcase and chop finely; keep aside. Melt the fat in a pan and fry the onion very gently until soft but not coloured. Stir in the flour and cook for 1 minute. Gradually add the stock and bring to the boil. Add salt, pepper, celery, salt, coriander and milk, cover and simmer for about 15 minutes. Add the chopped pheasant and cream, adjust the seasonings and reheat gently. Just before serving, stir in the tarragon. Hand the fried croutons separately.
SERVES 5-6

Croutons:
Cut 2-3 slices crustless bread into 1-2cm/$^{1}/_{2}$-$^{3}/_{4}$in cubes. Melt 50g/2oz butter in a pan with 3-4 tablespoons oil and 1-2 crushed cloves of garlic, if liked. When hot, add the bread and fry gently until golden brown, turning frequently.

Drain on absorbent paper and serve warm or cold.

Game soup recipes

VENISON SOUP

A good rich, meaty soup.

**Approx 1.3kg/3lb venison bones
with a little meat attached
1.75 litres/3 pints water
1 bouquet garni
2 carrots, peeled and sliced
2 onions, peeled and sliced
50g/2oz butter or margarine
50g/2oz flour
4 tablespoons sherry
1 tablespoon lemon juice
1 level tablespoon redcurrant jelly
2 level teaspoons tomato purée
Salt and pepper
Little gravy browning (optional)**

Brown the bones in a roasting tin in a hot oven (220°C/425°F, Gas Mark 7) for about 45 minutes. Transfer to a saucepan with any juices from the pan and add the water, bouquet garni, carrots and onions. Bring to the boil, cover and simmer gently for 2-3 hours or until a good rich stock. Strain and reserve 1.2 litres/2 pints stock and strip off any meat from the bones and mince or chop in a food processor with the carrots and onion.

In a clean pan melt the butter and stir in the flour. Cook for a minute or so, then gradually add the stock and bring up to the boil. Add the venison and vegetable mixture, sherry, lemon juice, redcurrant jelly, tomato purée and seasonings to taste. Return to the boil and simmer for about 15 minutes. Add gravy browning to give the desired rich brown colour and serve with fried croutons.
SERVES 6

Note: Suitable to freeze for up to 2 months.

CARROT AND PHEASANT SOUP

You need a good pheasant or other game stock for the base of this recipe together with chopped meat from the carcase to give a really tasty soup.

**50g/2oz butter or margarine
1 large onion, peeled and diced
900ml/1¹/2 pints good pheasant or game stock
1 level teaspoon ground coriander
Salt and pepper
2 tablespoons lemon juice
100-175g/4-6oz pheasant meat from the carcase, finely chopped
Approx 300ml/¹/2 pint milk or half cream**
To garnish:
**Snipped chives or fresh coriander
Single or double cream**

Melt the fat in the pan, add the onion and carrots and fry very gently for 10-15 minutes, stirring frequently, until soft, but in no way coloured. Add the stock and bring to the boil. Stir in the coriander plenty of salt and pepper, the lemon juice, cover and simmer for about 30 minutes or until the carrots are tender. Cool slightly then sieve, liquidise or purée in a food processor and return to a clean saucepan. Add the chopped pheasant meat and sufficient mild to give the required consistency. Bring slowly back to the boil and simmer for 2-3 minutes. Adjust the seasonings and serve with a tablespoon of cream swirled into the soup if liked, and topped with chives or coriander.
SERVES 4-6

Note: Suitable to freeze for up to 2 months, but add the cream when thawed and reheated.

TOMATO GAME SOUP

Use a carcase with plenty of meat still attached to it for the best results – but any gamebird will do.

1 pheasant carcase or 2-3 carcases of partridge, grouse etc
1.2 litres/2 pints water
Salt and pepper
1 bouquet garni
50g/2oz butter or margarine
1 onion, peeled and finely chopped
40g/1½ oz flour
½ level teaspoon curry powder (optional)
2 level tablespoons tomato purée
200g/7oz can sweetcorn kernels, drained
4-6 tomatoes, peeled and chopped
Good dash of Worcestershire sauce
Pinch of garlic powder
1 small red pepper, deseeded and chopped (optional)

Put the carcase into a saucepan with the water, salt, pepper and bouquet garni. Bring to the boil, skim and then cover and simmer for about 1½ hours, giving an occasional stir. Strain off the stock and reserve 1 litre/1¾ pints. Pick off as much meat from the carcase as you can and chop.

Melt the fat in a pan and fry the onion gently until soft. Stir in the flour, curry powder (if used) and the tomato purée and cook for a minute or so.

Gradually add the reserved stock and bring to the boil. Add the sweetcorn, tomatoes, Worcestershire sauce, garlic and chopped pheasant and simmer for about 15 minutes.

Add the chopped red pepper and continue to cook for a further 10 minutes. Adjust the seasonings and serve very hot.
SERVES 6

Note: Suitable to freeze for up to 2 months.

GAME SOUP WITH LENTILS

A substantial soup made with lentils, celery and carrots.

1-2 game carcases
1.75 litres/3 pints water
1 large onion, peeled and chopped
1 clove garlic, crushed
2-3 sticks celery, finely diced
2 carrots, finely diced
1 bay leaf
225g/8oz red lentils
4 tomatoes, peeled and chopped
Salt and pepper
1 potato, peeled and diced
1 tablespoon wine vinegar
To garnish:
Fried or toasted croutons
Chopped parsley

Break up the carcases and put into a saucepan with the water, onion, garlic, celery, carrots and bay leaf. Bring up to the boil, remove any scum from the surface and cover and simmer for 1-1½ hours. Remove the carcases and strip off any meat and chop.

Add the lentils to the stock with the tomatoes, seasonings, potato and vinegar. Bring back to the boil, cover and simmer for a further hour, giving an occasional stir. If liked, purée the soup, but it is better left chunky. Add the chopped reserved game meat and reheat. Adjust the seasonings and serve topped with croutons and chopped parsley.
SERVES 6-8

KNOW YOUR GAME
A guide to the main species

YOUNG or old? Male or female? Fresh or stale? Most people are familiar with the major game species, such as pheasant and hare, and those offered for sale by gamedealers and general butchers are usually well labelled. Lesser-known species may easily be identified by recourse to good textbooks and field guides. However, it is not always easy to distinguish male from female, and this can be important as some people have a clear preference for the meat of one or the other. But generally much more important than distinction between male and female is separation of young from old, for in most cases, excepting deer (the very young meat of which may be rather bland), the younger animal is preferred by the cook as being more tender.

Pheasant

Adult plumage is assumed quickly in this species and there is little danger of confusing the brightly coloured cock with the sombre brown hen. After trying a few birds, many people end up favouring the hen, as its meat is generally more tender, moist and delicate, but the larger cock offers better value. Note how the hen lays down much more fat to meet her breeding requirements.

Because of the way gameshooting is organised in Britain, with high turnover of birds and great reliance on rearing and release, most birds from big shoots will be of the year and thus should be relatively tender. A first-year cock will have short, rounded spurs without points. In his second year they are short but pointed. An old cock usually has long, sharp spurs.

A young hen has soft feet whereas an older bird has hard, rough feet. The hen's plumage may darken with age.

In both sexes the upper part of the yearling's beak is pliable. A young bird has the first primary (outer wing feather) pointed whereas an old bird's is rounded.

When buying pheasants, or any other gamebird, remember to feel the breast for plumpness, because although the price is usually the same for each brace (traditionally a male and female together), the weight of birds may vary considerably. Some apparently fat birds can be 'all feather'. Also, do not forget to ask your supplier when the birds came in because, if they are more than a day or two old, you could easily let them hang too long, especially if they have been in a damp or warm atmosphere about the shop.

As with most birds, pheasants are likely to be in top condition in autumn, when they are fully developed and had had the chance to feed well on a variety of nutritious foods throughout the summer and into October, when wild seeds and fruits are plentiful.

Partridge

Both the native grey or English and the introduced redlegged or French partridge are excellent eating, though among sportsmen there is an undoubted preference for the English, which has rather more flavour than the French. Both are reared widely, though nothing like to the extent of the pheasant programme, but the redleg is mostly confined to the drier climate of south-east England.

The cock and hen grey partridge are very similar but she is less boldly marked and her 'horseshoe' on the breast is generally fainter and sometimes missing. Her crown is more grey-white whereas the cock's is usually grey-brown. The juvenile grey has brown streaking where the adult is chestnut and is very similar to the juvenile redleg. In September and October the olive-yellow legs, dark beak and softer bones distinguish the young from the grey-legged, grey-beaked and hard-boned adults. Later in the season the young may be separated by the two outer primaries, which are pointed, but round-ended in the adult. If these feathers are pointed, but faded and worn, then the bird is in its second year. October partridges are usually about the best all round.

Redlegged partridge sexes are alike but the cock has knob-like spurs and is half an inch longer. Young redlegs resemble young greys before the adult plumage is acquired in November, except that they are rather more spotted than striped and lack the distinctive head pattern and barred flanks. The young also have the tips of the two outer primaries coloured cream.

Red grouse

If you see game for sale simply labelled 'grouse', then you can safely assume that it is the red grouse. Most are shot in northern Britain, where they live on the heather moors, but they are always available in London and many other towns and cities. The species is subject to considerable regional plumage variation, but generally the cock's comb above the eye is large and red whereas the hen's is smaller and pinker. She is paler and more heavily barred with lighter pigment whereas he has thinner, more wavy lines and spots. The hen has more yellow and brown mottling on the wings and dark tail. Both sexes adopt a winter plumage – the cock from mid-October and the hen from August.

The juvenile is like the hen. Its comb is less distinctive but cocks have chestnut under the chin and on the throat with little or no black barring, while in juvenile hens these feathers are generally yellower and the black barring is more pronounced. The grouse does not have spurs but there is a spur knob which is soft and rounded in the young but scaly and hard in the adult.

Young grouse have relatively bright eyes, smooth legs and soft, pliable feet. The tip of the breastbone is also soft and pliable. Older birds have hard, scaly feet, sharp claws and a hard breastbone. The young are more downy under the wing. In older birds the two outer primaries have rounded ends but those of the young are pointed in comparison with the other flight feathers. However, a second-year bird that has not moulted has these two feathers pointed but faded and tattered.

Grouse are in best condition from the start of the shooting season in August until mid-October. Most grouse are shot early in the season and supplies become more difficult later on.

Black grouse

The population and range of this magnificent bird have declined greatly this century. There is no danger of confusing the superb male – the blackcock – with the duller female – the greyhen. His average length is 21in, but her's only 16-17in.

Cocks take on winter plumage when only half-grown (from about mid-August), when they show patches of black and white but the tail is still only slightly curled and nothing like the lyre shape of the adults. The juvenile hen is like a small, dull adult female. As with red grouse, blackgame are in best condition during the first half of the season when feeding is easier.

Ptarmigan

A very distinctive bird, the adult of which always has white wings, though the rest of the plumage undergoes a series of seasonal changes for which the species is famous. This grouse lives on the Scottish mountain tops and its 'coats of many colours' are subject to considerable time variation, for the changes appear to be linked to temperature. Generally, from August to October, when most are shot, the male is pale grey and the female sandy grey. In winter dress from November to March, both sexes are all white except for the black on the tail, but the male can still be distinguished by the black mark between the beak and the eye.

The juvenile is like the autumn female but with pale-brown wings and tail, the same colour as the back. Usually only the oldest birds assume the pure-white dress so early as the end of the shooting season, the young occasionally retaining some grey feathers up to six weeks later.

Capercaillie

The massive cock bird is very different from the hen, which might be confused with the smaller greyhen. A young bird has supple feet with smooth, pliable legs. At first the juveniles of both sexes resemble the female, but the males adopt a dull adult plumage by the end of September.

Birds are in much better condition and fatter from September to early December. Later, cold weather will also deplete fat reserves more rapidly.

Woodcock

The sexes of this beautiful, mottled-brown bird are alike. The juvenile resembles the adult. Young birds have the primary tips ragged and worn whereas in older birds they are intact.

Woodcock are best from October to December before hard weather depletes their fat reserves, though even during that period some birds may be temporarily

A guide to the main species

emaciated after their long migration flight. If the vent is thin the bird is not in prime condition. An ideal bird will have a full breast, soft and supple feet and a clean mouth and throat.

Snipe

On the UK mainland we are concerned only with the common snipe, but in Ireland the smaller jack snipe is still legal quarry. The populations have declined alarmingly with land drainage, but both species are still widespread and common. The sexes are alike and the juvenile resembles the adult. With hatching sometimes continuing into August, there can be quite a few young around at the start of the shooting season. A young bird has softer feet, pointed wing feathers and a downy underwing.

These tiny birds are subject to rapid weight loss during hard weather, when they are frequently skinny. Thus they are generally in better condition up to November. As with the woodcock, if the bill is moist and the throat muddy then the bird has probably been dead for some time.

Golden plover

A beautiful wader which remains on the quarry list chiefly because of its great culinary value. The sexes are alike. The juvenile is of more uniform colour than the adult, darker below and paler above.

In good, fat condition a golden plover is hard at the vent, but if the vent is thin and flabby then the bird is a poor one. A young bird has soft, pliable feet.

Wild geese

In all species young birds may be recognised by the pliability of the underbill. Young also have softer limbs and windpipes. The tail feathers of immatures are notched whereas adults' are pointed, and the primaries of immatures are more liable to wear and fading and are pointed, whereas the adult's are more rounded until the summer moult.

The sexes are alike in appearance and flavour. The Canada is resident, but the other quarry geese are winter visitors. With all wildfowl – geese and ducks – fresh birds may be identified by their bright, full eyes.

Wild duck

In all quarry duck species the male and female have very different plumages and a good bird book will show you what they look like. However, they do also adopt eclipse plumages when confusion with young may arise.

Some species may still be in eclipse at the start of the shooting season. As far as flavour goes, there is no discernible difference between the sexes.

If you have a choice, always avoid wildfowl which are unduly muddy or badly shot-up as they will deteriorate more quickly.

The mallard is by far the most commonly eaten wild duck, often appearing on general sale in good, fat condition after coming from one of the many shoots where they are now hand-reared, released and fed throughout the winter.

The young bird is similar to the adult female. Advanced young may be distinguished early in the season by the tips of the tail feathers, which end with a notch where their downy tips have broken off. The adult's tail feathers are pointed.

In the wigeon, the juvenile resembles the female but is duller, particularly the wingbar, until February, when the plumage of the male assumes its rich colourings. This largely coastal duck is often best early in the season, especially where it has been feeding inland.

Moulting and juvenile male teal resemble the female, but with darker, more uniform upperparts. The juvenile's underparts are more spotted. Complete or partial eclipse in both sexes occurs from July to October, but full plumage has mostly returned by the end of September. Though small, the delicious teal is generally a plump bird and surprisingly able to maintain condition during frost.

Woodpigeon

The sexes are very much alike but the female is marginally smaller and duller. The woodpigeon has a very long breeding season, with young fledgling from March to October, but mostly June to August. Young birds are a prized dish. The fledged juvenile resembles the adult but is duller, tinged brown and without iridescence. The white neck ring starts to appear at about two months and is usually complete within a fortnight. The eyes change colour with age: in the young they are nearly black and in the adult brilliant yellow. A young pigeon has a plump breast but relatively thin thighs. Its legs are pinky-orange without scales and the claws are pinkish, but the adult has purple-red legs and toes and dark-brown claws. The juvenile has paler skin and the beak looks disproportionately large. Although the plumage is complete after the first moult it continues to develop intensity of colour.

Hare

The brown hare is distinguished from the rabbit by its longer black-tipped ears, longer legs and greater size. Its ears are longer than those of the mountain or blue hare. The fur is yellow-brown and the upper surface of the tail dark. The mountain hare has grey-brown fur, which sometimes turns white in winter, and the upper surface of its tail is white. It is smaller and stockier than the brown hare.

For cooking it is well worthwhile trying to get a young hare. Juveniles have small, white teeth, soft and thin ears, smooth coats and claws hidden by fur, and the small 'nut' on the paw is well developed. The younger the hare the sharper the claws. As a hare gets older the claws become rounded and rough and project slightly, the teeth grow long, yellow and irregular, and the cleft in the jaw is more obvious. The 'hare lip' is quite narrow in the young leveret but becomes wider with age. Also with age white hairs appear on the muzzle, the coat becomes more wavy with traces of grey and the ears become tough, dry and hard. A stiff-bodied hare is fresh but a limp one is stale.

Rabbit

As with the hare, the sexes are alike but the smaller female has a narrower head and her profile from ears to nose is slightly less rounded than in the male. The hind feet are much shorter than those of both hare species, and the tips of the ears are brown.

A rabbit is best at about 3-4 months old, when it is plump and has a lot of white fat around the kidneys. A young rabbit's eyes are bright, its claws smooth and

feet flexible. Its ears tear easily and the lower jaw yields to pressure between thumb and forefinger.

Deer

For the purposes of this book, distinction between male and female is not really necessary, and in any case it is unlikely that anyone other than an expert stalker will wish to handle a whole carcase. In most households only joints are likely to be encountered.

Unfortunately, some butchers do not even know the species of deer. Also, in order to identify a young animal it is necessary to see the unskinned carcase, though obviously a small joint is likely to come from a younger animal, allowing for size variation among species.

However, very young deer are sometimes rejected by experienced cooks who say that the meat lacks flavour.

A red deer does not attain fully maturity until seven years old. It is generally suckled for 8-10 months and the milk teeth are completely replaced by 26 months. Red deer venison is more widely available in northern Britain, though there are herds in the south-west and an increasing number of deer farms.

Fallow males reach puberty at 7-14 months and females first breed at 16 months – also the approximate age at which a roe deer attains adult size (soon after puberty).

Salmon

When they first run up the rivers salmon are usually in good condition as they are fresh from their feeding grounds at sea and the presence of sea-lice is regarded as a good thing. Then this king of fish is silvery and graceful with firm, red flesh and tissue well stocked with fat.

During spawning this fat is extended and the flesh becomes pale and watery, the skin darkened, and in the males the front teeth become enlarged, the lower jaw hooked and the snout prolonged.

The skin of the back becomes thick and spongy with scales embedded in it. These are known as red fish and the darker females black fish. Kelt is the general term applied to both in this spent condition. Most of these fish soon die. Size does not truly reflect age as a fish

The main species/The seasons

which has spent more time at sea feeding will be bigger. Average length is $16^1/2$-$37^1/2$in (40-90cm), but specimens grow to 50in (120cm).

In the sea both sexes have a green-blue back, silvery sides, spotted back and white belly, but in fresh water the male (cock) has a green-brown back, sides brownish or pink with black spots edged pink or orange, fins dark blue-grey or brown and the lower jaw often hooked. The female (hen) lacks the pink tint and hooked jaw.

Brown trout

Trout are very variable in form and colour, but generally this species achieves a length of $8^1/2$-21in (20-50cm). However, while the brown trout is among the most variably coloured fish it never has a prominent band of colour along each side, as the rainbow trout has. Its spots are orange or red but those of the rainbow are black only.

Rainbow trout

Average length is 10-$18^1/2$in (25-45cm) but 29in (70cm) may be reached. Rainbow trout are so widely available now that stale fish are unlikely to be encountered.

Sea-trout

This beautiful trout is sometimes misleadingly called 'salmon-trout' on the fishmonger's slab, no doubt to attract a higher price, but the misrepresentation is unnecessary as the flesh of this fish is second to none.

Unlike the other trout, the sea-trout is migratory. Its size averages 10-25in (25-60cm) but occasionally it reaches 37.5in (90cm). The colour is silvery blue-green with a darker back and white belly. The sides and back are sparsely spotted with dark-blue or black and there are spots on the dorsal and caudal fins and operculum.

The colour and intensity of the male's spots increase during spawning, when he develops a hooked jaw. In fact they can be hard to tell from a salmon, but the salmon has a thinner stem to the tail and the rear edge of the tail fin is usually more or less forked whereas that of the sea-trout is fairly straight. The upper jawbone of the sea-trout extends to, and often beyond, the rear of the eye, but that of the salmon rarely reaches this far. The sea-trout has 13-16 scales between the adipose fin and the lateral line but the salmon has 10-13. The front of the salmon's vomer (small bone separating the nostrils) is toothless but that of the sea-trout has teeth.

THE SEASONS

The shooting or 'taking' of quarry species, including those classified as 'game', is strictly controlled by law, particularly by the Wildlife and Countryside Act 1981, its subsequent amendments, and the various Game Acts. The dates given below are inclusive and refer to Britain and Ireland, except where indicated.

Grouse	August 12-December 10
Partridge	September 1-February 1
Pheasant	October 1-February 1
Ptarmigan	August 12-December 10
Blackgame	August 20-December 10
Capercaillie	October 1-January 31
Common Snipe	August 12-January 31
Woodcock	October 1-January 31
	(Scotland: September 1-January 31)
Hare	No close season
Wild geese and duck in or over any area below High Water Mark of ordinary Spring Tides:	September 1-February 20
Elsewhere:	September 1-January 31
Golden Plover	September 1-January 31

DEER CLOSE SEASONS

		England-Wales	Scotland
Red	Stags	May 1-July 31	Oct 21-June 30
	Hinds	March 1-Oct 31	Feb 16-Oct 20
Fallow	Buck	May 1-July 31	May 1-July 31
	Doe	March 1-Oct 31	Feb 16-Oct 20
Roe	Buck	Nov 1-Mar 31	Oct 21-Mar 31
	Doe	Mar 1-Oct 31	April 1-Oct 20
Sika	Stags	May 1-July 31	Oct 21-June 30
	Hinds	March 1-Oct 31	Feb 16-Oct 20

Salmon and Trout
There are no national close seasons as such for salmon and trout but somewater authorities have their own open seasons, which are chiefly from early spring to autumn. Some stillwaters permit winter trout fishing.